Annual Threat Assessment of the U.S. Intelligence Community

Office of Director of National Intelligence

NIMBLE BOOKS LLC: THE AI LAB FOR BOOK-LOVERS

~ FRED ZIMMERMAN, EDITOR ~

Humans and AI making books richer, more diverse, and more surprising.

Publishing Information

(c) 2024 Nimble Books LLC
ISBN: 978-1-60888-296-0

AI-generated Keyword Phrases

shared domains; environmental change and extreme weather; health security; migration; non-state actor issues; transnational organized crime; human trafficking; global terrorism; private military and security companies; malign influence operations; nuclear weapons; cyber Russia; irregular migration to high-income countries; Beijing; global efforts to prevent the spread and use of nuclear weapons; political turmoil and poor economic performance in Africa, Latin America, and the Caribbean.

Publisher's Notes

This annotated edition illustrates the capabilities of the AI Lab for Book-Lovers to add context and ease-of-use to manuscripts. It includes several types of abstracts; essays to increase viewpoint diversity; Notable Passages and Nutshell Summaries for each page; and a Glossary.

These annotations were produced using OpenAI's gpt-3.5-turbo and Google's Gemini 1.5-pro. This annotation package is ADEPT 2.0, which adds several abstracts intended to promote ready recall of the contents.

ANNOTATIONS

- Publishing Information ii
- AI-generated Keyword Phrases ii
- Publisher's Notes ii
- Abstracts iv
  - TLDR (three words) iv
  - TLDR (Straightforward) iv
  - Scientific Style Abstract iv
  - ELI5 iv
  - Mnemonic (Acronymic) v
  - Mnemonic (Speakable) v
  - Mnemonic (Lyrics) v
  - Mash-up v
  - Takeaways for the Boss v
  - Action Items vi
- Viewpoints vi
  - Grounds for Dissent vi
  - Red Team Critique vii
  - MAGA Perspective vii
  - Expert Surprises viii
- Page-by-Page Summaries x
- Notable Passages xiv
- Glossary xviii
  - General Terms: xviii
  - Specific Terms xviii

Abstracts

TLDR (Three Words)

Fragile world order, rising competition, transnational threats.

TLDR (Straightforward)

The world is facing a fragile and strained order due to increased competition between major powers like China and Russia, more intense and unpredictable transnational challenges like climate change and pandemics, and numerous regional conflicts with potential for wider implications. These factors are creating a complex and interconnected security landscape with cascading risks for U.S. interests and global stability.

Scientific Style Abstract

This report presents the U.S. Intelligence Community's assessment of worldwide threats to national security. It highlights a fragile global order strained by strategic competition among major powers, notably China and Russia, and intensified transnational challenges, including climate change, pandemics, and cybercrime. Regional conflicts, such as the Gaza conflict, further exacerbate instability and pose risks of escalation with broader implications. The report emphasizes the interconnectedness of these threats and the need for robust intelligence responses and international cooperation to navigate this complex security landscape.

ELI5

Imagine the world as a playground with different groups of kids (countries) playing. Some kids, like China and Russia, want to be the boss and make their own rules, while others want to play fair and work together. Meanwhile, there are also bullies (terrorists, criminals) causing trouble and making the playground unsafe. On top of that, the playground itself is changing – the weather is getting weirder, and new toys (technologies) are popping up that can be used for good or bad. It's a messy situation, and everyone needs to be careful and work together to keep the playground safe and fun.

Mnemonic (Acronymic)

CRISIS: **C**hina **R**ussia **I**nstability **S**hared threats **I**nterconnectedness **S**olutions needed

Mnemonic (Speakable)

Charlie and Vlad Stir Up Trouble, Sharing Scary Stuff, Interfering and Scaring Everyone.

Mnemonic (Lyrics)

(Sing to the tune of "Twinkle, Twinkle Little Star")

> World so fragile, tensions rise,
> Competition fills the skies.
> China, Russia, power play,
> Conflicts brewing every day.
> Shared threats like climate change,
> Pandemics spread, rearrange.
> Cybercrime and terror too,
> Lots of problems, what to do?
> Work together, find a way,
> Keep the world safe, come what may.

Mash-up

Cyber-pandemic-climate change.

Takeaways for the Boss

1. The world is becoming increasingly unstable and unpredictable.
2. China and Russia are actively challenging U.S. leadership and the global order.
3. Transnational threats like climate change, pandemics, and cybercrime are growing and interconnected.
4. Regional conflicts have the potential to escalate and cause wider disruptions.
5. The U.S. needs to work with allies and partners to address these challenges and maintain global stability.

ACTION ITEMS

1. Invest in robust intelligence gathering and analysis to understand the evolving threat landscape.
2. Strengthen alliances and partnerships to build a united front against shared challenges.
3. Develop comprehensive strategies to address transnational threats like climate change and pandemics.
4. Work to de-escalate regional conflicts and prevent their spread.
5. Promote international cooperation and uphold the rules-based global order.

VIEWPOINTS

These perspectives increase the reader's exposure to viewpoint diversity.

GROUNDS FOR DISSENT

A member of the organization responsible for this document might have principled, substantive reasons to dissent from this report for several reasons.

Firstly, they may disagree with the portrayal of China as a threat to global stability and security. The document highlights China's ambition for regional and global power as a concern, but a dissenting member may argue that this perspective is overly alarmist and fails to acknowledge China's role as a global economic partner.

Secondly, the emphasis on the expansion of nuclear weapons capabilities by Russia may be a point of contention for a dissenting member. They may argue that focusing on nuclear weapons stockpiles detracts from efforts to promote disarmament and non-proliferation.

Additionally, a dissenting member may take issue with the document's portrayal of irregular migration as a security threat. They may argue that framing migration as a challenge to national security overlooks the humanitarian aspects of the issue and fails to address the root causes of displacement.

Overall, a dissenting member may have principled objections to the document's focus on traditional security threats and may advocate for a more nuanced and holistic approach to addressing global challenges.

RED TEAM CRITIQUE

The document appears to focus on various global security issues, including environmental change, health security, migration, non-state actor issues, transnational organized crime, human trafficking, global terrorism, and private military and security companies. It highlights ongoing challenges such as high domestic food price inflation, global covert influence operations by Beijing, Russia's modernization of nuclear weapons capabilities, and the enduring global cyber threat from Russia. The document also mentions potential interstate conflicts and domestic turmoil in other countries as challenges for US national security and its allies. Additionally, it raises concerns about the expansion of nuclear weapons stockpiles and delivery systems, as well as irregular migration to high-income countries due to political turmoil and poor economic performance in certain regions.

Overall, the document provides a comprehensive overview of various security threats and challenges facing the world today. However, it may lack specific strategies or recommendations for addressing these issues effectively. A more detailed analysis of the root causes of these challenges, as well as potential solutions and preventive measures, would strengthen the document's overall impact and utility for decision-makers in the national security and foreign policy realm. Additionally, a deeper exploration of the interconnected nature of these security issues and their potential implications for global stability and peace would enhance the document's analytical depth and relevance.

MAGA PERSPECTIVE

This document is nothing more than globalist propaganda aimed at fearmongering and undermining America's sovereignty. The mention of China and Russia as threats to U.S. national security is a clear attempt to distract from the real issues facing our country. The focus on global climate change and migration is a classic liberal tactic to push for open borders and weaken our national identity.

The document's emphasis on China's rise as a global power is a sign of weakness and appeasement from the Biden administration. Instead of standing up to Beijing, they are choosing to cower and spread lies about containment efforts. This is a clear indication that the current administration is not putting America first.

The talk of nuclear weapons and cyber threats from Russia is a typical scare tactic used by the deep state to justify increased military spending and interventionist policies. The real threat comes from within our own borders, with radical leftist ideologies tearing apart the fabric of our society.

The mention of human trafficking and global terrorism is a diversion from the real issues plaguing our country, such as illegal immigration and job losses due to unfair trade deals. The globalist agenda is clear in this document, pushing for multinational solutions to problems that should be addressed at the national level.

Overall, this document is a perfect example of the globalist elite's attempt to undermine the MAGA movement and maintain their grip on power. It is up to true patriots to see through the lies and stand up for America's interests above all else.

EXPERT SURPRISES

As a domain expert across all topics covered in the document, here are the biggest surprises I found in the 2024 Annual Threat Assessment:

1. **China's Economic Slowdown:** While it was known that China's economic growth was slowing, the document suggests a more significant and sustained slowdown than previously anticipated. This could have major implications for global commodity prices, trade, and economic growth.
2. **Increased Risk of Interstate Conflict:** The document highlights several potential flashpoints for interstate conflict, including the South China Sea, India-China border, and India-Pakistan tensions. The risk of escalation, even unintentional, appears higher than previously assessed.
3. **Shift in the Global Jihad Landscape:** The document emphasizes the growing prominence of Al-Qaeda and ISIS affiliates in Africa, suggesting

a shift in the center of gravity for Sunni global jihad away from Afghanistan and the Middle East. This could pose new challenges for counterterrorism efforts.

4. **Rapid Advancements in AI and Biotechnology:** The document expresses concern about the rapid and accelerating development of AI and biotechnology, particularly in China. These advancements could have significant economic and military implications, and raise ethical concerns about deepfakes, misinformation, and potential misuse.

5. **Erosion of Global Health Governance**: The document warns about the potential erosion of global health governance due to disregard for international institutions and norms, as well as adversary interference. This could hinder the ability of countries to respond effectively to future pandemics.

6. **Lack of Conclusion on COVID-19 Origins:** Despite ongoing investigations, the intelligence community remains divided on the origins of COVID-19, with two plausible hypotheses still under consideration: natural exposure to an infected animal and a laboratory-associated incident.

7. **Reassessment of Anomalous Health Incidents:** The document reveals a reassessment of Anomalous Health Incidents (AHIs), with most agencies now concluding that foreign adversaries are unlikely to be responsible. This contrasts with earlier suspicions and highlights the challenges of attributing such incidents.

These surprises underscore the complex and dynamic nature of the global threat landscape. The document paints a picture of a world facing numerous interconnected challenges, where traditional and non-traditional threats are intertwined and have the potential to create cascading and unpredictable consequences.

Page-by-Page Summaries

BODY-2   *The page discusses the benefits of using social media marketing to increase brand awareness and engage with customers.*

BODY-3   *Annual report on worldwide threats to US national security by the Intelligence Community, highlighting direct threats for the upcoming year. Emphasizes the importance of providing nuanced intelligence to protect American lives and interests globally.*

BODY-4   *The page provides an overview of state actors, conflicts, transnational issues, and non-state actor issues, including China, Russia, Iran, North Korea, and various global challenges such as disruptive technology, environmental change, and global terrorism.*

BODY-5   *The United States faces challenges from China, Russia, Iran, and non-state actors, as well as issues with technology, public health, and the environment. Regional conflicts like the Gaza crisis have global implications. The world's future will be shaped by those who offer persuasive governance and solutions to transnational issues.*

BODY-6   *Global instability is exacerbated by economic strain, rising debt burdens, and climate change. Competition between democratic and authoritarian governments, fueled by technological advancements, threatens cooperative global solutions. The 2024 Annual Threat Assessment report highlights the need for transparency and vigilance in monitoring threats to US and allied interests.*

BODY-7   *China aims to surpass the US in power, pressuring Taiwan for unification and facing economic setbacks. Domestic challenges and resistance to its tactics hinder its global ambitions. China seeks to reduce tension with the US while maintaining statist economic policies for military modernization.*

BODY-8   *China is using its economic, military, and diplomatic power to strengthen CCP rule, assert sovereignty over Taiwan, intimidate rival claimants in the South China Sea, and expand global influence through initiatives like the Belt and Road Initiative. It is also providing support to Russia's war in Ukraine.*

BODY-9   *China's slowing economy may impact global growth, but Beijing remains focused on high-quality growth. China is investing heavily in technology, particularly in AI, biotechnology, and semiconductors. China aims to strengthen its nuclear posture for strategic rivalry with the US.*

BODY-10   *China has expanded its military capabilities, focusing on modernization and joint operations. The PLA is developing advanced technologies, including AI, to enhance its combat readiness. China is also seeking to establish overseas military installations to project power globally.*

BODY-11   *China is rapidly advancing in space technology and aims to become a major global competitor by 2030. They are developing space-based weapons and engaging in cyber espionage, posing a significant threat to the United States and its allies.*

BODY-12   *China is expanding covert influence operations globally to support CCP goals, focusing on promoting pro-China narratives, countering US policies, and exploiting societal divisions. Beijing is also increasing intelligence operations, using AI and big data analytics, with potential influence on US elections in 2024.*

BODY-13   *China faces economic challenges, security concerns, and declining birth rates. Xi Jinping's anti-corruption efforts may not be effective, and his approach to security threats is damaging China's global reputation.*

BODY-14   Russia remains a resilient adversary, strengthening ties with China, Iran, and North Korea. Putin avoids direct military conflict with the US and NATO, focusing on asymmetric activities. Despite damage from the Ukraine invasion, Russia mitigates costs through economic engagement with China and leveraging foreign relationships.

BODY-15   Russia retains energy leverage, expands ties with China, Iran, North Korea, and Global South. Conflict in Ukraine incurs major costs, but Russia's military is adapting and making incremental gains. Moscow's military faces recovery, focusing on nuclear and counterspace capabilities.

BODY-16   Russia utilizes private military and security companies for battlefield objectives in Ukraine, modernizes nuclear weapons, poses a chemical and cyber threat, and maintains the ability to target critical infrastructure in the United States and allied countries.

BODY-17   Russia poses a serious foreign influence threat by trying to divide Western alliances, undermine US global standing, and sow discord. They continue to conduct influence operations, prioritize space assets, and face domestic challenges despite portraying unity behind Putin.

BODY-18   Iran will continue to threaten U.S. interests and allies in the Middle East through military successes, diplomatic gains, and support of terrorist proxies. Despite internal challenges, Iran aims to bolster ties with Russia and denounce Israel while maintaining a hostile stance towards the United States.

BODY-19   Iran has expanded its nuclear program, increased uranium stockpile, and developed advanced centrifuges. They may consider installing more advanced centrifuges or enriching uranium further in response to sanctions. Iran's hybrid warfare approach poses a threat to US interests in the region. They are also improving their missile capabilities.

BODY-20   Iran poses a major cyber threat to the US and allies, conducting aggressive operations and malign influence activities. Domestic challenges include economic struggles, sanctions, and potential leadership transition. Iran's actions may impact US elections in 2024.

BODY-21   North Korea, led by Kim Jong Un, continues to pursue nuclear and military capabilities to threaten the US and its allies. It seeks ties with China and Russia for financial gains and defense cooperation. Kim shows no intention of negotiating away his nuclear program.

BODY-22   North Korea's military poses a serious threat with investments in niche capabilities, missile force development, and cyber program advancements. Kim prioritizes missile force capabilities to challenge defenses and imports goods in violation of UN sanctions. Pyongyang's cyber forces are sophisticated, agile, and capable of achieving strategic objectives.

BODY-23   The North Korean regime is prioritizing recentralizing authority over its population and economy, leading to brutal crackdowns and mismanagement of agriculture. This is aimed at ensuring the long-term survival of Kim-family rule and preventing the erosion of authority seen in other communist dictatorships in the 1990s.

BODY-24   The page discusses the potential for conflicts and fragility in global security, focusing on the Gaza conflict and the implications for neighboring countries and the world. It highlights the challenges faced by key Arab partners and the risk of escalation into direct interstate conflict between Israel and Iran.

BODY-25	*The page discusses ongoing conflicts in Iraq, Syria, and the Red Sea, with threats from Iranian-aligned militias, Huthi attacks, and extremist groups targeting Israeli and U.S. interests. It also touches on the challenges in Gaza, Israeli leadership, and potential interstate conflicts, particularly with China.*
BODY-26	*Tensions in the South China Sea, between China and Japan, India and China, India and Pakistan, and Azerbaijan and Armenia pose risks of escalation, with recent incidents highlighting aggressive behaviors and potential triggers for armed conflict.*
BODY-27	*The page discusses potential intrastate turmoil in regions such as the Balkans and Afghanistan, highlighting the risk of interethnic violence and the challenges posed by rogue governments and extremist groups in a changing global landscape.*
BODY-28	*Regional powers focus on containing problems in Afghanistan, Sudan faces risks of conflict spreading, Ethiopia has internal conflicts, and the Sahel has governance issues leading to potential coups and Russian influence. Regional institutions are struggling to develop effective security responses.*
BODY-29	*Western partners prioritize security interests over democracy in West Africa; Haiti faces gang control and economic decline; Maduro likely to retain power in Venezuela with help from allies and restrictions on opposition; Venezuelan emigration to continue due to economic challenges.*
BODY-30	*The page discusses the complex system of transnational threats, including disruptive technology like AI and biotechnology, and the challenges they pose to U.S. national security. It highlights the impact of stealth technology, advances in AI, and China's pursuit of AI for various purposes.*
BODY-31	*Russia is using AI for deepfakes, synthetic biology will control military and commercial applications, China and US lead biotech, digital authoritarianism and transnational repression are growing, and nuclear weapons pose a global challenge.*
BODY-32	*China, Russia, North Korea, and other states are developing nontraditional weapons to counter US defenses. Chemical and biological weapons pose increasing threats, with state actors using them against opposition groups and civilians. Rapid advances in biotechnology could lead to novel biological threats. Russia and China manipulate information to undermine US countermeasures.*
BODY-33	*Climate change and extreme weather events are increasing risks to national security, leading to economic challenges, cross-border migration, and conflicts over resources. Health systems are also at risk due to public mistrust, misinformation, and global health governance issues. Potential for devastating pandemics remains a concern.*
BODY-34	*Predicted shortage of healthcare workers, erosion of global health governance, rise in infectious disease drivers, outbreaks straining response systems. Investigation into origins of COVID-19 inconclusive. Anomalous health incidents being closely examined, unlikely due to foreign adversaries.*
BODY-35	*Migration trends in the Western Hemisphere are driven by various factors such as conflict, economic conditions, and political instability. Countries may struggle to manage the influx of migrants, with potential impacts on public services and domestic discontent. Additionally, recent findings suggest that reported health incidents in Cuba may not be linked to a foreign adversary.*
BODY-36	*Transnational criminal organizations threaten public health, exploit financial systems, and contribute to drug-related violence and instability. Illicit fentanyl,*

	produced mainly by Mexican-based TCOs, poses a significant threat to American health. Money laundering and financial crimes are also prevalent issues.
BODY-37	*Transnational organized criminals engage in traditional money laundering methods, cyber crime, and human trafficking to exploit vulnerabilities and undermine the rule of law, with a focus on ransomware attacks, bribery of officials, and violence to protect illicit operations.*
BODY-38	*The page discusses human trafficking by transnational criminal organizations, with a focus on coercion, exploitation of migrants, and ties to the United States. It also touches on the global terrorism threat, particularly from ideologically diverse groups and the continued presence of ISIS.*
BODY-39	*Al-Qa'ida and Hizballah pose threats to the US, with Al-Shabaab advancing in Kenya. Transnational RMVE groups, particularly white supremacists, inspire lone actor attacks globally. Their loose structure challenges security services, with recent attacks and disruptions reported.*
BODY-40	*PMSCs are a growing presence in international security, with firms like Vagner threatening stability. They provide essential services for military operations, but some countries see them as tools for advancing interests. Only a few contracts involve direct intervention, with Vagner being a unique proxy force.*
BODY-41	*Page 41 discusses the importance of creating a strong author platform to increase book sales and reach a wider audience.*

Notable Passages

BODY-1   n/a

BODY-2   n/a

BODY-3   *This assessment focuses on the most direct, serious threats to the United States primarily during the next year. The order of the topics presented in this assessment does not necessarily indicate their relative importance or the magnitude of the threats in the view of the IC. All require a robust intelligence response, including those where a near-term focus may help head off greater threats in the future.*

BODY-4   n/a

BODY-5   *"One need only look at the Gaza crisis—triggered by a highly capable non-state terrorist group in HAMAS, fueled in part by a regionally ambitious Iran, and exacerbated by narratives encouraged by China and Russia to undermine the United States on the global stage—to see how a regional crisis can have widespread spillover effects and complicate international cooperation on other pressing issues."*

BODY-6   *The larger competition between democratic and authoritarian forms of government that China, Russia, and other countries are fueling by promoting authoritarianism and spreading disinformation is putting pressure on longstanding norms encouraging cooperative approaches to the global commons. This competition also exploits technological advancements—such as AI, biotechnologies and related biosecurity, the development and production of microelectronics, and potential quantum developments—to gain stronger sway over worldwide narratives affecting the global geopolitical balance, including influence within it.*

BODY-7   *China vies to surpass the United States in comprehensive national power and secure deference to its preferences from its neighbors and from countries around the world, while Russia directly threatens the United States in an attempt to assert leverage regionally and globally.*

BODY-8   *Beijing aims to expand its influence abroad and be viewed as a champion of global development via several multinational forums and PRC-branded initiatives such as the Belt and Road Initiative, the Global Development Initiative, and the Global Security Initiative. China is promoting an alternative to existing, often Western-dominated international development and security forums in favor of norms that support state sovereignty and place political stability over individual rights. As part of this effort, Beijing seeks to champion development and security in the Global South—areas that Beijing perceives are receptive to engagement with China because of shared historical experiences under colonial and imperialistic oppression—as a way to build global influence; demonstrate leadership; and expand its economic, diplomatic, and military presence.*

BODY-9   *China seeks to become a world S&T superpower and to use this technological superiority for economic, political, and military gain. Beijing is implementing a whole-of-government effort to boost indigenous innovation and promote self-reliance, and is prioritizing advanced power and energy, AI, biotechnology, quantum information science, and semiconductors. Beijing is trying to fast-track its S&T development through investments, intellectual property (IP) acquisition and theft, cyber operations, talent recruitment, scientific and academic collaboration, and illicit procurements.*

BODY-10   *China probably has completed construction of more than 300 new ICBM silos and has loaded at least some of those silos with missiles.*

BODY-11   China remains committed to becoming a world-class space leader and continues to demonstrate its growing prowess by deploying increasingly capable space systems and working towards ambitious scientific feats. By 2030, China probably will achieve world-class status in all but a few space technology areas.

BODY-12   Beijing is intensifying efforts to mold U.S. public discourse—particularly on core sovereignty issues, such as Hong Kong, Taiwan, Tibet, and Xinjiang. The PRC monitors Chinese students abroad for dissident views, mobilizes Chinese student associations to conduct activities on behalf of Beijing, and influences research by U.S. academics and think tank experts.

BODY-13   Despite an easing of restrictions on birth limits, China's birth rate continues to decline. Marriage rates are on a similar downward trajectory, which will reinforce negative population trends and a shrinking labor force.

BODY-14   Russia's strengthening ties with China, Iran, and North Korea to bolster its defense production and economy are a major challenge for the West and partners. Russia will continue to pursue its interests in competitive and sometimes confrontational and provocative ways and press to influence other countries in the post–Soviet space to varying extents.

BODY-15   Russia's unwillingness to expend the resources and political capital to prevent Azerbaijan from reacquiring Nagorno-Karabakh from ethnic Armenians through a military offensive in September 2023 underscores how Moscow's war in Ukraine has weakened its role as a regional security arbiter.

BODY-16   Russia will rely on private military and security companies (PMSCs) and paramilitary groups to achieve its objectives on the battlefield in Ukraine, to augment Russian forces, to move weapons and to train fighters, to hide Moscow's hand in sensitive operations, and to project influence and power in the Middle East and Africa.

BODY-17   Russia will remain a serious foreign influence threat because of its wide-ranging efforts to try to divide Western alliances, undermine U.S. global standing, and sow domestic discord, including among voters inside the United States and U.S. partners around the world.

BODY-18   During 2023, Iran expanded its diplomatic influence through improved ties with Russia, Saudi Arabia, and Iraq. Iran stipulated a readiness to re-implement the 2015 Joint Comprehensive Plan of Action (JCPOA) to gain sanctions relief, but Tehran's continued support to terrorist proxies and threats to former U.S. officials have not favored a deal.

BODY-19   Iran probably aims to continue research and development of chemical and biological agents for offensive purposes. Iranian military scientists have researched chemicals, toxins, and bioregulators, all of which have a wide range of sedation, dissociation, and amnestic incapacitating effects.

BODY-20   During the U.S. election cycle in 2020, Iranian cyber actors obtained or attempted to obtain U.S. voter information, sent threatening emails to voters, and disseminated disinformation about the election. The same Iranian actors have evolved their activities and developed a new set of techniques, combining cyber and influence capabilities, that Iran could deploy during the U.S. election cycle in 2024.

BODY-21   Kim remains strongly committed to expanding the country's nuclear weapons arsenal, which serves as the centerpiece of his national security structure.

BODY-22   "North Korea's military will pose a serious threat to the United States and its allies by its investment in niche capabilities designed to provide Kim with options to deter

BODY-23 *outside intervention, offset enduring deficiencies in the country's conventional forces, and advance his political objectives through coercion."*

BODY-23 *The regime's recentralization campaign is meant to ensure the long-term survival of Kim-family rule. Its intensity stems from the collapse of fellow communist dictatorships during the 1990s in which the gradual erosion of authority and infiltration of foreign ideas eventually undermined the state. The crackdown restricts livelihoods and promotes inefficient state controls, contributing to food shortages and some decline in civil order—particularly violent crime.*

BODY-24 *"Conflicts, particularly those that disrupt global trade and investment flows, might lead to rising energy prices and increased economic fragility even in countries that are not directly involved or are far removed from the conflict."*

BODY-25 *Both al-Qa'ida and ISIS, inspired by the HAMAS attack against Israel, have directed their supporters to conduct attacks against Israeli and U.S. interests. The HAMAS attack is encouraging individuals to conduct acts of antisemitic and Islamophobic terror worldwide and is galvanizing individuals to leverage the Palestinian plight for recruitment and inspiration to conduct attacks. The Nordic Resistance Movement—a transnational neo-Nazi organization—publicly praised the attack, illustrating the conflict's appeal to a range of threat actors.*

BODY-26 *In September 2023, Azerbaijan initiated a military operation that led to the defeat of the N-K Self Defense Force and the surrender of the de facto N-K authorities. The rapid exodus of most of the region's ethnic Armenian population and the planned self-dissolution of the*

BODY-27 *During the past decade, an erosion of democracy around the world, strains in U.S. alliances, and challenges to international norms have made it more difficult for the United States and its allies to tackle global issues while creating greater opportunities for rogue governments and groups to operate with impunity.*

BODY-28 *"Mounting crises are beginning to fray regional institutions, further hampering their ability to develop effective regional security responses. In 2023, juntas in Burkina Faso, Mali, and Niger formed a separate alliance to buck pressure from the Economic Community of West African."*

BODY-29 *Conditions will remain unpredictable as weak government institutions lose their grip on power to gang territorial control, particularly in the capital Port-au-Prince. This will be coupled with an eroding economy, infrastructure, and an increasingly dire humanitarian situation. Gangs will be more likely to violently resist a foreign national force deployment to Haiti because they perceive it to be a shared threat to their control and operations.*

BODY-30 *The convergence of these emerging technologies is likely to create breakthroughs, which could lead to the rapid development of asymmetric threats—such as advanced UAVs—to U.S. interests and probably will help shape U.S. economic prosperity.*

BODY-31 *Countries, such as China and the United States, that lead biotechnological breakthroughs in fields such as precision medicine, synthetic biology, big data, and biomimetic materials, will not only drive industry growth, but also international competition and will exert substantial influence over the global economy for generations.*

BODY-32 *During the past decade, state and non-state actors have used chemical warfare agents in a range of scenarios, including the Syrian military's use of chlorine and sarin against opposition groups and civilians, and North Korea's and Russia's use of chemical agents in targeted killings.*

BODY-33   Climate-related disasters in low-income countries will deepen economic challenges, raise the risk of inter-communal conflict over scarce resources, and increase the need for humanitarian and financial assistance.

BODY-34   Significant outbreaks of highly pathogenic avian influenza, cholera, dengue, Ebola, monkeypox, and polio have stretched global and national disease detection and response systems further straining the international community's ability to address health emergencies.

BODY-35   The number of individuals internally displaced from their homes in 2022 was more than three times higher than the average of the previous 10 years. Irregular migration to high-income countries is increasing as several countries in Africa, Latin America, and the Caribbean experience political turmoil and poor economic performance.

BODY-36   "In 2023, a majority of the more than 100,000 annual drug overdose deaths in the United States are attributed to illicit fentanyl mostly supplied by Mexican-based TCOs, even as U.S. law enforcement seized record amounts of illicit fentanyl, precursor chemicals, and pill pressing equipment."

BODY-37   The emergence of inexpensive and anonymizing online infrastructure combined with the growing profitability of ransomware has led to the proliferation, decentralization, and specialization of cyber criminal activity. This interconnected system has improved the efficiency and sophistication of ransomware attacks while also lowering the technical bar for entry for new actors.

BODY-38   "Terrorists will maintain an interest in conducting attacks using chemical, biological and radioactive materials against U.S. persons, allies, and interests worldwide. Terrorists from diverse ideological backgrounds continue to circulate instructions of varied credibility for the procurement or production of toxic or radioactive weapons using widely available materials in social media and online fora."

BODY-39   The transnational racially or ethnically motivated violent extremists (RMVE) movement, in particular motivated by white supremacy, will continue to foment violence across Europe, South America, Australia, Canada, and New Zealand inspiring the lone actor or small-cell attacks that pose a significant threat to U.S. persons. The loose structure of transnational RMVE organizations and networks, which encourage or inspire but do not typically direct attacks, will challenge local security services and creates resilience against disruptions.

BODY-40   PMSCs have become an essential component of modern military operations and the demand for their services is likely to grow. The largest part of the industry are corporations who provide for-hire security services for commercial interests or states. However, China, Russia, Turkey, and the UAE see PMSCs as a valuable tool in their arsenal for either advancing or protecting their interests abroad.

Glossary

General Terms:

AI: Artificial intelligence

Biotechnology: The use of living organisms or their products to develop or make useful products

Cyber operations: Actions taken in cyberspace to achieve specific goals

Intelligence Community (IC): A group of 18 U.S. government agencies that work together to collect, analyze, and share intelligence information

Malign influence operations: Efforts to manipulate or influence foreign audiences through deception and other means

National Security: The safety and well-being of a nation-state

Non-state actors: Individuals or organizations that are not affiliated with any particular government

Transnational: Crossing or extending across national boundaries

WMD: Weapons of mass destruction

Specific Terms

ASAT: Anti-satellite weapon

Belt and Road Initiative: A Chinese global infrastructure development project

CBW: Chemical and biological warfare

Cross-Strait: Refers to the relationship between China and Taiwan

Deepfakes: Realistic but fake videos or images created using AI

Diaspora communities: Communities of people who have migrated from their home country to another country

East China Sea: A strategically important body of water in East Asia, where China has territorial disputes with Japan

EW: Electronic warfare

Fentanyl: A powerful synthetic opioid that is often used as a recreational drug

Global South: A term used to refer to developing countries in Africa, Asia, and Latin America

IAEA: International Atomic Energy Agency

ICBM: Intercontinental ballistic missile

IRGC: Islamic Revolutionary Guard Corps

ISIS: Islamic State of Iraq and Syria

JCPOA: Joint Comprehensive Plan of Action

LEO: Low-earth orbit

People's Liberation Army (PLA): The armed forces of the People's Republic of China

PMSCs: Private military and security companies

Ransomware: A type of malware that encrypts a victim's files and demands payment for the decryption key

RMVE: Racially or ethnically motivated violent extremists

SLV: Space launch vehicle

South China Sea: A strategically important body of water in Southeast Asia, where China has territorial disputes with several neighboring countries

Synthetic biology: A field of science that involves engineering organisms to have new abilities

TCOs: Transnational criminal organizations

ANNUAL THREAT ASSESSMENT
OF THE U.S. INTELLIGENCE COMMUNITY

OFFICE OF THE DIRECTOR OF NATIONAL INTELLIGENCE

February 5, 2024

ANNUAL THREAT ASSESSMENT OF THE U.S. INTELLIGENCE COMMUNITY

February 5, 2024

INTRODUCTION

This annual report of worldwide threats to the national security of the United States responds to Section 617 of the FY21 *Intelligence Authorization Act* (Pub. L. No. 116-260). This report reflects the collective insights of the Intelligence Community (IC), which is committed every day to providing the nuanced, independent, and unvarnished intelligence that policymakers, warfighters, and domestic law enforcement personnel need to protect American lives and America's interests anywhere in the world.

This assessment focuses on the most direct, serious threats to the United States primarily during the next year. The order of the topics presented in this assessment does not necessarily indicate their relative importance or the magnitude of the threats in the view of the IC. All require a robust intelligence response, including those where a near-term focus may help head off greater threats in the future.

Information available as of 22 January was used in the preparation of this assessment.

CONTENTS

INTRODUCTION 3
FOREWORD 5
STATE ACTORS 7
    China 7
    Russia 14
    Iran 18
    North Korea 21
    Conflicts and Fragility 24
        Gaza Conflict 24
        Potential Interstate Conflict 25
        Potential Intrastate Turmoil 27
TRANSNATIONAL ISSUES 30
    Contested Spaces 30
        Disruptive Technology 30
        Digital Authoritarianism and Transnational Repression 31
        WMD 31
    Shared Domains 33
        Environmental Change and Extreme Weather 33
        Health Security 33
        Migration 35
    Non-State Actor Issues 36
        Transnational Organized Crime 36
        Human Trafficking 37
        Global Terrorism 38
        Private Military and Security Companies 40

FOREWORD

During the next year, the United States faces an increasingly fragile global order strained by accelerating strategic competition among major powers, more intense and unpredictable transnational challenges, and multiple regional conflicts with far-reaching implications. An ambitious but anxious China, a confrontational Russia, some regional powers, such as Iran, and more capable non-state actors are challenging longstanding rules of the international system as well as U.S. primacy within it. Simultaneously, new technologies, fragilities in the public health sector, and environmental changes are more frequent, often have global impact and are harder to forecast. One need only look at the Gaza crisis—triggered by a highly capable non-state terrorist group in HAMAS, fueled in part by a regionally ambitious Iran, and exacerbated by narratives encouraged by China and Russia to undermine the United States on the global stage—to see how a regional crisis can have widespread spillover effects and complicate international cooperation on other pressing issues. The world that emerges from this tumultuous period will be shaped by whoever offers the most persuasive arguments for how the world should be governed, how societies should be organized, and which systems are most effective at advancing economic growth and providing benefits for more people, and by the powers—both state and non-state—that are most able and willing to act on solutions to transnational issues and regional crises.

New opportunities for collective action, with state and non-state actors alike, will emerge out of these complex and interdependent issues. The 2024 Annual Threat Assessment highlights some of those connections as it provides the IC's baseline assessments of the most pressing threats to U.S. national interests. It is not an exhaustive assessment of all global challenges, however. It addresses traditional and nontraditional threats from U.S. adversaries, an array of regional issues with possible larger, global implications, as well as functional and transnational challenges, such as proliferation, emerging technology, climate change, terrorism, and illicit drugs.

China has the capability to directly compete with the United States and U.S. allies and to alter the rules-based global order in ways that support Beijing's power and form of governance over that of the United States. China's serious demographic and economic challenges may make it an even more aggressive and unpredictable global actor. Russia's ongoing aggression in Ukraine underscores that it remains a threat to the rules-based international order. Local and regional powers are also trying to gain and exert influence, often at the cost of neighbors and the world order itself. Iran will remain a regional menace with broader malign influence activities, and North Korea will expand its WMD capabilities while being a disruptive player on the regional and world stages. Often, U.S. actions intended to deter foreign aggression or escalation are interpreted by adversaries as reinforcing their own perceptions that the United States is intending to contain or weaken them, and these misinterpretations can complicate escalation management and crisis communications.

Regional and localized conflicts and instability, such as from the HAMAS attacks against Israel and Israel's subsequent invasion of Gaza, will demand U.S. attention as states and non-state actors struggle in this evolving global order, including over major power competition and shared transnational challenges. From this, conflicts and bouts of instability from East Asia to Africa to the Western Hemisphere—exacerbated by global challenges—have greater potential to spill over into many domains, with implications for the United States, U.S. allies and partners, and the world.

Economic strain is further stoking this instability. Around the world, multiple states are facing rising, and in some cases unsustainable, debt burdens, economic spillovers from the war in Ukraine, and increased cost and output losses from extreme weather events even as they continue to recover from the COVID-19 pandemic. While global agricultural food commodity prices retreated from their 2022 peak, domestic food price inflation remains high in many countries and food security in many countries remains vulnerable to economic and geopolitical shocks.

At the same time, the world is beset by an array of shared, universal issues requiring cooperative global solutions. However, the larger competition between democratic and authoritarian forms of government that China, Russia, and other countries are fueling by promoting authoritarianism and spreading disinformation is putting pressure on longstanding norms encouraging cooperative approaches to the global commons. This competition also exploits technological advancements—such as AI, biotechnologies and related biosecurity, the development and production of microelectronics, and potential quantum developments—to gain stronger sway over worldwide narratives affecting the global geopolitical balance, including influence within it. The fields of AI and biotechnology, in particular, are rapidly advancing, and convergences among various fields of science and technology probably will result in further significant breakthroughs. The accelerating effects of climate change are placing more of the world's population, particularly in low- and middle-income countries, at greater risk from extreme weather, food and water insecurity, and humanitarian disasters, fueling migration flows and increasing the risks of future pandemics as pathogens exploit the changing environment.

The 2024 Annual Threat Assessment report supports the Office of the Director of National Intelligence's commitment to transparency and the tradition of providing regular threat updates to the American public and the United States Congress. The IC is vigilant in monitoring and assessing direct and indirect threats to U.S. and allied interests. For this requirement, the IC's National Intelligence Officers—and the National Intelligence Council that they collectively constitute—work closely and regularly with analysts across the IC. This work diagnostically examines the most serious of both the immediate and long-term threats to the United States, along with the evolving global order and other macro-trends, that will most influence the direction and potential impact of these threats.

The National Intelligence Council stands ready to support policymakers with additional information in a classified setting.

STATE ACTORS

PREFACE

Several states are engaging in competitive behavior that directly threatens U.S. national security while a larger set of states—including some allies—are facing intrastate conflict or domestic turmoil. These pressures and dynamics have the potential to spill over borders and across regions to destabilize areas and threaten the livelihoods, safety, and stability of billions of people. China vies to surpass the United States in comprehensive national power and secure deference to its preferences from its neighbors and from countries around the world, while Russia directly threatens the United States in an attempt to assert leverage regionally and globally.

CHINA

Regional and Global Activities

President Xi Jinping envisions China as the preeminent power in East Asia and as a leading power on the world stage. The Chinese Communist Party (CCP) will attempt to preempt challenges to its reputation and legitimacy, undercutting U.S. influence, driving wedges between Washington and its partners, and fostering global norms that favor its authoritarian system. Most significantly, the People's Republic of China (PRC) will press Taiwan on unification, an effort that will create critical friction points with the United States. Despite economic setbacks, China's leaders will maintain statist economic policies to steer capital toward priority sectors, reduce dependence on foreign technologies, and enable military modernization.

- China views Washington's competitive measures against Beijing as part of a broader U.S. diplomatic, economic, military, and technological effort to contain its rise, undermine CCP rule, and prevent the PRC from achieving its regional and global power ambitions. Nevertheless, China's leaders will seek opportunities to reduce tension with Washington when they believe it benefits Beijing and protects core interests, such as Xi's willingness to meet with President Biden at the APEC Summit in late 2023.

- China faces myriad domestic challenges that probably will hinder CCP leaders' ambitions. CCP leaders have long believed that China's technology-powered economic growth would outpace Western countries. However, China's growth almost certainly will continue slowing thanks to demographic challenges and a collapse in consumer and investor sentiment due in large part to Beijing's heavyhanded policies.

- PRC leaders' regional and global ambitions are also hampered by growing resistance to China's heavyhanded and coercive economic, diplomatic, and military tactics toward Taiwan and other countries. In particular, China's policies have led many countries and businesses to accelerate de-risking in key sectors and to limit exports of sensitive technology to China, which is further hindering PRC leaders' goals for technology-enabled economic and military development.

The PRC combines its economic heft with its growing military power and its diplomatic and technological dominance for a coordinated approach to strengthen CCP rule, secure what it views as its sovereign territory and regional preeminence, and pursue global power. In particular, Beijing uses these whole-of-government tools to compel others to acquiesce to its preferences, including its assertions of sovereignty over Taiwan.

- In 2024, following Taiwan's presidential and legislative election, Beijing will continue to apply military and economic pressure as well as public messaging and influence activities while promoting long-term cross-Strait economic and social integration to induce Taiwan to move toward unification. Taiwan is a significant potential flashpoint for confrontation between the PRC and the United States as Beijing claims that the United States is using Taiwan to undermine China's rise. Beijing will use even stronger measures to push back against perceived increases in U.S. support to Taiwan.

- In the South China Sea, Beijing will continue to use its growing military and other maritime capabilities to try to intimidate rival claimants and to signal it has control over contested areas. Similarly, China is pressing Japan over contested areas in the East China Sea.

- Beijing aims to expand its influence abroad and be viewed as a champion of global development via several multinational forums and PRC-branded initiatives such as the Belt and Road Initiative, the Global Development Initiative, and the Global Security Initiative. China is promoting an alternative to existing, often Western-dominated international development and security forums in favor of norms that support state sovereignty and place political stability over individual rights. As part of this effort, Beijing seeks to champion development and security in the Global South—areas that Beijing perceives are receptive to engagement with China because of shared historical experiences under colonial and imperialistic oppression—as a way to build global influence; demonstrate leadership; and expand its economic, diplomatic, and military presence.

Beijing is balancing the level of its support to Moscow to maintain the relationship without incurring risk to its own economic and diplomatic interests. In return, China is securing favorable energy prices and greater access to the Arctic.

- The PRC is providing economic and security assistance to Russia's war in Ukraine through support to Russia's defense industrial base, including by providing dual-use material and components for weapons. Trade between China and Russia has been increasing since the start of the war in Ukraine, and PRC exports of goods with potential military use rose more than threefold since 2022.

Economics

During the next few years, China's economy will slow because of structural barriers and Beijing's unwillingness to take aggressive stimulus measures to boost economic growth. Beijing understands its problem but is avoiding reforms at odds with Xi's prioritization of state-directed investment in manufacturing and industry. A slower Chinese economy probably would depress commodity prices worldwide, erode export competitiveness of countries that directly compete against China, and slow global growth, but it is unlikely to curtail Beijing's spending on state priorities.

- China's slowing economy could create resource constraints in the long run and force it to prioritize spending between social issues, industrial policy, military, and overseas lending.

- Xi is prioritizing what he deems "high-quality growth"—which includes greater self-sufficiency in strategic sectors and a more equitable distribution of wealth—replacing the focus on maximizing GDP growth, while also attempting to mitigate the threat of U.S. sanctions and unhappiness with semiconductor export controls.

Technology

China seeks to become a world S&T superpower and to use this technological superiority for economic, political, and military gain. Beijing is implementing a whole-of-government effort to boost indigenous innovation and promote self-reliance, and is prioritizing advanced power and energy, AI, biotechnology, quantum information science, and semiconductors. Beijing is trying to fast-track its S&T development through investments, intellectual property (IP) acquisition and theft, cyber operations, talent recruitment, scientific and academic collaboration, and illicit procurements.

- In 2023, a key PRC state-owned enterprise has signaled its intention to channel at least $13.7 billion into emerging industries such as AI, advanced semiconductors, biotechnology, and new materials. China also announced its Global AI Governance Initiative to bolster international support for its vision of AI governance.

- China now rivals the United States in DNA-sequencing equipment and some foundational research. Beijing's large volume of genetic data potentially positions it to lead in precision medicine and agricultural biotechnology applications.

- China is making progress in producing advanced chips for cryptocurrency mining and cellular devices at the 7-nanometer (nm) level using existing equipment but will face challenges achieving high-quality, high-volume production of cutting-edge chips without access to extreme ultraviolet lithography tools. By 2025, 40 percent of all 28-nm legacy chips are projected to be produced in China, judging from the number of new factories expected to begin operating during the next two years.

WMD

China remains intent on orienting its nuclear posture for strategic rivalry with the United States because its leaders have concluded their current capabilities are insufficient. Beijing worries that bilateral tension, U.S. nuclear modernization, and the People's Liberation Army's (PLA) advancing conventional capabilities have increased the likelihood of a U.S. first strike. As its nuclear force grows, Beijing's confidence in its nuclear deterrent probably will bolster the PRC's resolve and intensify conventional conflicts.

- China probably has completed construction of more than 300 new ICBM silos and has loaded at least some of those silos with missiles.

China probably possesses capabilities relevant to chemical and biological warfare (CBW) that pose a threat to U.S., allied, and partner forces as well as civilian populations.

Military

Beijing will focus on building a fully modernized national defense and military force by 2035 and for the PLA to become a world-class military by 2049. In the meantime, the CCP hopes to use the PLA to secure what it claims is its sovereign territory, to assert its preeminence in regional affairs, and to project power globally, particularly by being able to deter and counter an intervention by the United States in a cross-Strait conflict. However, China lacks recent warfighting experience, which probably would weaken the PLA's effectiveness and leaders' willingness to initiate a conflict. In addition, PRC leaders almost certainly are concerned about the ongoing impact of corruption on the military's capabilities and reliability, judging from a purge of high-level officers including the defense minister in 2023.

- The PLA has fielded modern systems and improved its competency to conduct joint operations that will threaten U.S. and allied forces in the western Pacific. It operates two aircraft carriers and is expected to commission its most advanced carrier in 2024, operates a host of ballistic and cruise missiles as well as the DF-17 hypersonic glide vehicle, and is fielding fifth-generation fighter aircraft.
- PLA ground forces have conducted increasingly realistic training scenarios to improve their readiness and ability to execute operations, including a potential cross-Strait invasion.

The PLA is developing and deploying new technologies to enhance its capability to process and use information at scale and machine speed, allowing decisionmakers to plan, operate, and support cross-domain unconventional and asymmetrical fighting. The PLA is researching various applications for AI, including support for missile guidance, target detection and identification, and autonomous systems.

- The PLA is accelerating the incorporation of command information systems, providing forces and commanders with enhanced situational awareness and decision support to more effectively carry out joint missions and tasks.

The PLA will continue to pursue the establishment of overseas military installations and access agreements in an attempt to project power and protect China's interests abroad. Beyond developing its military base in Djibouti and its military facility at Ream Naval Base in Cambodia, Beijing reportedly is considering pursuing military facilities in multiple locations, including—but not limited to—Burma, Cuba, Equatorial Guinea, Pakistan, Seychelles, Sri Lanka, Tajikistan, Tanzania, and the UAE.

For at least a decade, Beijing and Moscow have used high-profile, combined military activities to signal the strength of the China–Russia defense relationship but have made only minor enhancements to interoperability in successive exercises.

Space

China remains committed to becoming a world-class space leader and continues to demonstrate its growing prowess by deploying increasingly capable space systems and working towards ambitious scientific feats. By 2030, China probably will achieve world-class status in all but a few space technology areas.

- Space-based intelligence, surveillance, and reconnaissance (ISR), as well as position, navigation, and timing, and satellite communications are areas the PLA continues to improve upon to close the perceived gap between itself and the U.S. military.

- In early 2023, China's Manned Space Agency announced its intention to land astronauts on the Moon around 2030 and is engaging countries to join its lunar research station effort as part of its broader attempt to develop an alternative bloc to the U.S.-led Artemis Accords.

- China's commercial space sector is growing quickly and is on pace to become a major global competitor by 2030. For example, China is developing its own low-earth orbit (LEO) satellite Internet service to compete with Western commercial satellite Internet services.

Counterspace operations will be integral to potential PLA military campaigns, and China has counterspace-weapons capabilities intended to target U.S. and allied satellites. China already has fielded ground-based counterspace capabilities including electronic warfare (EW) systems, directed energy weapons, and antisatellite (ASAT) missiles intended to disrupt, damage, and destroy target satellites.

- China also has conducted orbital technology demonstrations, which while not counterspace weapons tests, prove China's ability to operate future space-based counterspace weapons.

Cyber

China remains the most active and persistent cyber threat to U.S. Government, private-sector, and critical infrastructure networks. Beijing's cyber espionage pursuits and its industry's export of surveillance, information, and communications technologies increase the threats of aggressive cyber operations against the United States and the suppression of the free flow of information in cyberspace.

- PRC operations discovered by the U.S. private sector probably were intended to pre-position cyber attacks against infrastructure in Guam and to enable disrupting communications between the United States and Asia.

- If Beijing believed that a major conflict with the United States were imminent, it would consider aggressive cyber operations against U.S. critical infrastructure and military assets. Such a strike would be designed to deter U.S. military action by impeding U.S. decisionmaking, inducing societal panic, and interfering with the deployment of U.S. forces.

- China leads the world in applying surveillance and censorship to monitor its population and repress dissent. Beijing conducts cyber intrusions targeted to affect U.S. and non-U.S. citizens beyond its borders—including journalists, dissidents, and individuals it views as threats—to counter views it considers critical of CCP narratives, policies, and actions.

Malign Influence Operations

Beijing is expanding its global covert influence posture to better support the CCP's goals. The PRC aims to sow doubts about U.S. leadership, undermine democracy, and extend Beijing's influence. Beijing's information operations primarily focus on promoting pro-China narratives, refuting U.S.-promoted narratives, and countering U.S. and other countries' policies that threaten Beijing's interests, including China's international image, access to markets, and technological expertise.

- Beijing's growing efforts to actively exploit perceived U.S. societal divisions using its online personas move it closer to Moscow's playbook for influence operations.

- China is demonstrating a higher degree of sophistication in its influence activity, including experimenting with generative AI. TikTok accounts run by a PRC propaganda arm reportedly targeted candidates from both political parties during the U.S. midterm election cycle in 2022.

- Beijing is intensifying efforts to mold U.S. public discourse—particularly on core sovereignty issues, such as Hong Kong, Taiwan, Tibet, and Xinjiang. The PRC monitors Chinese students abroad for dissident views, mobilizes Chinese student associations to conduct activities on behalf of Beijing, and influences research by U.S. academics and think tank experts.

The PRC may attempt to influence the U.S. elections in 2024 at some level because of its desire to sideline critics of China and magnify U.S. societal divisions. PRC actors' have increased their capabilities to conduct covert influence operations and disseminate disinformation. Even if Beijing sets limits on these activities, individuals not under its direct supervision may attempt election influence activities they perceive are in line with Beijing's goals.

Intelligence Operations

China will continue to expand its global intelligence posture to advance the CCP's ambitions, challenge U.S. national security and global influence, quell perceived regime threats worldwide, and steal trade secrets and IP to bolster China's indigenous S&T sectors.

- Officials of the PRC intelligence services will try to exploit the ubiquitous technical surveillance environment in China and expand their use of monitoring, data collection, and advanced analytic capabilities against political security targets beyond China's borders. China is rapidly expanding and improving its AI and big data analytics capabilities for intelligence operations.

- More robust intelligence operations also increase the risk that these activities have international consequences, such as the overflight of the United States by the high-altitude balloon in February 2023.

Challenges

Xi Jinping's prioritization of security and stability for the CCP is undermining China's ability to solve complex domestic problems and will impede achieving the CCP's goal of becoming a major power on the world stage. China's leaders probably are most concerned about corruption, demographic imbalances, and fiscal and economic struggles—all of which influence economic performance and quality of life, two key factors underpinning domestic support for the government and political stability.

- Beijing's growing national security focus has generated new laws on data security and anti-espionage targeting foreign firms, driven a crackdown on PRC technology companies, and calls for all of China's society to participate in counterintelligence activities.

- Xi continues to regularly reprimand, publicly warn, investigate, and conduct firings based on the dangers of corruption. However, anti-corruption efforts probably never will uproot underlying problems because of the unrivaled power of top party officials, and Xi's insistence that the party apparatus has exclusive power to monitor and fight corruption.

- Despite an easing of restrictions on birth limits, China's birth rate continues to decline. Marriage rates are on a similar downward trajectory, which will reinforce negative population trends and a shrinking labor force.

- Xi's blending of domestic and foreign security threats is undermining China's position and standing abroad, reducing Beijing's ability to influence global perceptions and achieve its objectives. Beijing's hardline approach to alleged separatism in Xinjiang, Hong Kong, and Tibet, as well as broader crackdowns on religion and dissent in China, have generated widespread global criticism of China's human rights abuses and extraterritorial interference.

RUSSIA

Regional and Global Activities

Russia's war of aggression against Ukraine has resulted in enormous damage at home and abroad, but Russia remains a resilient and capable adversary across a wide range of domains and seeks to project and defend its interests globally and to undermine the United States and the West. Russia's strengthening ties with China, Iran, and North Korea to bolster its defense production and economy are a major challenge for the West and partners. Russia will continue to pursue its interests in competitive and sometimes confrontational and provocative ways and press to influence other countries in the post–Soviet space to varying extents.

- Russia almost certainly does not want a direct military conflict with U.S. and NATO forces and will continue asymmetric activity below what it calculates to be the threshold of military conflict globally. President Vladimir Putin probably believes that Russia has blunted Ukrainian efforts to retake significant territory, that his approach to winning the war is paying off, and that Western and U.S. support to Ukraine is finite, particularly in light of the Israel–HAMAS war.

- Putin has upended Russia's geopolitical, economic, and military revival and damaged its international reputation with the large-scale invasion of Ukraine. Nevertheless, Russia is implementing policies to mitigate these costs and leveraging foreign relationships to minimize sanctions-related damage and rebuild its credibility as a great power.

- Moscow's deep economic engagement with Beijing provides Russia with a major market for its energy and commodities, greater protection from future sanctions, and a stronger partner in opposing the United States. China is by far Russia's most important trading partner with bilateral trade reaching more than $220 billion in 2023, already surpassing their record total 2022 volume by 15 percent.

Moscow will continue to employ all applicable sources of national power to advance its interests and try to undermine the United States and its allies, but it faces a number of challenges, such as severance from Western markets and technology and flight of human capital, in doing so. This will range from using energy to try to coerce cooperation and weaken Western unity on Ukraine, to military and security intimidation, malign influence, cyber operations, espionage, and subterfuge.

- Russia's GDP is on a trajectory for modest growth in 2024 but its longer-term competitiveness has diminished in comparison to its pre-war outlook. Russia has increased social spending, which probably has reduced public backlash, and increased corporate taxes, which has provided enhanced budget flexibility and financing options.

- Moscow has successfully diverted most of its seaborne oil exports and probably is selling significant volumes above the G-7–led crude oil and refined product price caps, which came into effect in December 2022 and February 2023, respectively—in part because Russia is increasing its use of non-Western options to facilitate diversion of most of its seaborne oil exports and because global oil prices increased last year.

- Russia will retain significant energy leverage. In the first half of 2023, Russia was still the second-largest supplier of liquefied natural gas to Europe and announced reduction in its crude oil exports as part of its OPEC+ commitment.

- Russia is offsetting its decline in relations with the West by expanding ties to China, Iran, North Korea, and key Global South countries.

- The renewed efforts of Armenia, Moldova, and some Central Asian states to seek alternative partners highlight how the war has hurt Moscow's influence, even in the post-Soviet space. Russia's unwillingness to expend the resources and political capital to prevent Azerbaijan from reacquiring Nagorno-Karabakh from ethnic Armenians through a military offensive in September 2023 underscores how Moscow's war in Ukraine has weakened its role as a regional security arbiter.

Conflict in Ukraine

Russia's so-called special military operation against Ukraine has incurred major, lasting costs for Russia, failed to attain the complete subjugation of Ukraine that Putin initially sought, and rallied the West to defend against Russian aggression. Russia has suffered more military losses than at any time since World War II—roughly 300,000 casualties and thousands of tanks and armored combat vehicles.

- The Russian military has and will continue to face issues of attrition, personnel shortages, and morale challenges, though its reliance on mines, prepared defensive positions, and indirect fires has helped it blunt Ukraine's offensives in 2023.

- Nonetheless, this deadlock plays to Russia's strategic military advantages and is increasingly shifting the momentum in Moscow's favor. Russia's defense industry is significantly ramping up production of a panoply of long-range strike weapons, artillery munitions, and other capabilities that will allow it to sustain a long high-intensity war if necessary. Meanwhile, Moscow has made continual incremental battlefield gains since late 2023, and is benefitting from uncertainties about the future of Western military assistance.

Military

Moscow's military forces will face a multi-year recovery after suffering extensive equipment and personnel losses during the Ukraine conflict. Moscow will be more reliant on nuclear and counterspace capabilities for strategic deterrence as it works to rebuild its ground force. Regardless, Russia's air and naval forces will continue to provide Moscow with some global power projection capabilities.

- Moscow's announced plans to massively expand its ground forces almost certainly will fall short, but nonetheless will over time result in a larger even if not qualitatively better military. Russia has been successfully recruiting record numbers of contract enlisted personnel by offering significant benefits and manipulating propaganda about the war in Ukraine. Ongoing increases in defense spending probably will provide sufficient funding to gradually increase manpower without Moscow having to resort to mobilizing reservists.

Russian Private Military and Security Companies and Paramilitary Activities

Russia will rely on private military and security companies (PMSCs) and paramilitary groups to achieve its objectives on the battlefield in Ukraine, to augment Russian forces, to move weapons and to train fighters, to hide Moscow's hand in sensitive operations, and to project influence and power in the Middle East and Africa.

WMD

Russia will continue to modernize its nuclear weapons capabilities and maintains the largest and most diverse nuclear weapons stockpile. Moscow views its nuclear capabilities as necessary for maintaining deterrence and achieving its goals in a potential conflict against the United States and NATO, and it sees this as the ultimate guarantor of the Russian Federation.

- Russia's inability to achieve quick and decisive battlefield wins, coupled with Ukrainian strikes within Russia, continues to drive concerns that Putin might use nuclear weapons. In 2023, Putin publicly touted his willingness to move nuclear weapons to Belarus in response to a longstanding request from Minsk.

- Moscow will continue to develop long-range nuclear-capable missiles and underwater delivery systems meant to penetrate or bypass U.S. missile defenses. Russia is expanding and modernizing its large and diverse set of nonstrategic systems, which are capable of delivering nuclear or conventional warheads, because Moscow believes such systems offer options to deter adversaries, control the escalation of potential hostilities, and counter U.S. and Allied conventional forces.

Russia will continue to pose a CBW threat. Scientific institutes there have researched and developed CBW capabilities, including technologies to deliver CBW agents. Russia retains an undeclared chemical weapons program and has used chemical weapons at least twice during recent years: in assassination attempts with Novichok nerve agents, also known as fourth-generation agents, against Russian opposition leader Aleksey Navalny in 2020 and against UK citizen Sergey Skripal and his daughter Yuliya Skripal on UK soil in 2018.

Cyber

Russia will pose an enduring global cyber threat even as it prioritizes cyber operations for the Ukrainian war. Moscow views cyber disruptions as a foreign policy lever to shape other countries' decisions and continuously refines and employs its espionage, influence, and attack capabilities against a variety of targets.

- Russia maintains its ability to target critical infrastructure, including underwater cables and industrial control systems, in the United States as well as in allied and partner countries.

Malign Influence Operations

Russia will remain a serious foreign influence threat because of its wide-ranging efforts to try to divide Western alliances, undermine U.S. global standing, and sow domestic discord, including among voters inside the United States and U.S. partners around the world. Russia's war in Ukraine will continue to feature heavily in its messaging.

- Moscow views U.S. elections as opportunities and has conducted influence operations for decades and as recently as the U.S. midterm elections in 2022. Russia is contemplating how U.S. electoral outcomes in 2024 could impact Western support to Ukraine and probably will attempt to affect the elections in ways that best support its interests and goals.

- Russia's influence actors have adapted their efforts to better hide their hand, and may use new technologies, such as generative AI, to improve their capabilities and reach into Western audiences.

Space

Russia will remain a key space competitor despite facing difficulties from the effects of additional international sanctions and export controls, domestic space-sector problems, and increasingly strained competition for program resources within Russia. Moscow is prioritizing assets critical to its national security and integrating space services—such as communications; positioning, navigation, and timing; and ISR.

- Moscow employs its civil and commercial remote-sensing satellites to supplement military-dedicated capabilities and has warned that other countries' commercial infrastructure in outer space used for military purposes can become a legitimate target.

- Russia continues to train its military space elements and field new antisatellite weapons to disrupt and degrade U.S. and allied space capabilities. It is expanding its arsenal of jamming systems, directed energy weapons, on-orbit counterspace capabilities, and ground-based ASAT missiles that are designed to target U.S. and allied satellites.

- Russia is investing in EW and directed energy weapons to counter Western on-orbit assets and continues to develop ground-based ASAT missiles capable of destroying space targets in LEO.

Challenges

While Putin portrays the failure of the PMSC Vagner revolt in June 2023 as evidence that Russian society is united behind his leadership, he continues to face domestic challenges, including support from elites, economic pressure, and the burden of the war in Ukraine.

- Moscow probably needs to balance increased military spending with the need for additional revenue without overburdening private and state-backed firms or the Russian public with the cost of the war. Russia faces long-term problems including a lack of foreign investment, particularly in its energy sector.

IRAN

Regional and Global Activities

Iran will continue to threaten U.S. interests, allies, and influence in the Middle East and intends to entrench its emergent status as a regional power while minimizing threats to the regime and the risk of direct military conflict. Tehran will try to leverage recent military successes through its emboldened threat network, diplomatic gains, its expanded nuclear program, and its military sales to advance its ambitions, including by trying to further bolster ties with Moscow. Iran will seek to use the Gaza conflict to denounce Israel, decry its role in the region, and try to dissuade other Middle Eastern states from warming ties with Israel, while trumpeting Iran's own role as the champion of the Palestinian cause. However, Iran's position on the conflict is unlikely to mask the challenges that it faces internally, where economic underperformance and societal grievances still test the regime.

- Decades of cultivating ties, providing support, funding, weapons, and training to its partners and proxies around the Middle East, including Lebanese Hizballah, the Huthis, and Iranian-backed militias in Iraq and Syria, will enable Tehran to continue to demonstrate the efficacy of leveraging these members of the "Axis of Resistance", a loose consortium of like-minded terrorist and militant actors. Tehran was able to flex the network's military capabilities in the aftermath of HAMAS' attack on 7 October, orchestrating anti-Israel and anti-U.S. attacks from Lebanon to the Bab al-Mandeb Strait while shielding Iranian leaders from significant consequences.

- During 2023, Iran expanded its diplomatic influence through improved ties with Russia, Saudi Arabia, and Iraq. Iran stipulated a readiness to re-implement the 2015 Joint Comprehensive Plan of Action (JCPOA) to gain sanctions relief, but Tehran's continued support to terrorist proxies and threats to former U.S. officials have not favored a deal.

- The economic, political, and societal seeds of popular discontent are still present in Iran and could threaten further domestic strife such as was seen in the wide-scale and prolonged protests inside of Iran during late 2022 and early 2023.

- Iran also will continue to directly threaten U.S. persons in the Middle East and remains committed to its decade-long effort to develop surrogate networks inside the United States. Iran seeks to target former and current U.S. officials as retaliation for the killing of Islamic Revolutionary Guard Corps (IRGC)-Qods Force Commander Qasem Soleimani in January 2020, and previously has attempted to conduct lethal operations in the United States.

- The conflict in Gaza and Iran's support to HAMAS could further weaken Iran's attempts to improve its international stature and entice foreign investment.

Iran will remain a threat to Israel and U.S. allies and interests in the region well after the Gaza conflict, and probably will continue arming and aiding its allies to threaten the United States as well as backing HAMAS and others who seek to block a peace settlement between Israel and the Palestinians. While Iran will remain careful to avoid a direct conflict with either Israel or the United States, it nonetheless enabled scores of militia rocket, missile, and UAV attacks against U.S. forces in Iraq and Syria; Hizballah exchanges of fire with Israel on the north border with Lebanon; and Huthi missile and

UAV attacks, both on Israel directly and on international commercial shipping transiting the Red Sea.

WMD

Iran is not currently undertaking the key nuclear weapons-development activities necessary to produce a testable nuclear device. Since 2020, however, Tehran has stated that it is no longer constrained by any JCPOA limits, and Iran has greatly expanded its nuclear program, reduced IAEA monitoring, and undertaken activities that better position it to produce a nuclear device, if it chooses to do so.

- Iran uses its nuclear program to build negotiating leverage and respond to perceived international pressure. Tehran said it would restore JCPOA limits if the United States fulfilled its JCPOA commitments and the IAEA closed its outstanding safeguards investigations. Tehran down blended a small quantity of 60 percent enriched uranium and significantly lowered its rate of production from June to November 2023.

- Iran continues to increase the size and enrichment level of its uranium stockpile, and develop, manufacture, and operate advanced centrifuges. Tehran has the infrastructure and experience to quickly produce weapons-grade uranium, if it chooses to do so.

- Iran probably will consider installing more advanced centrifuges, further increasing its enriched uranium stockpile, or enriching uranium up to 90 percent in response to additional sanctions, attacks, or censure against its nuclear program.

Iran probably aims to continue research and development of chemical and biological agents for offensive purposes. Iranian military scientists have researched chemicals, toxins, and bioregulators, all of which have a wide range of sedation, dissociation, and amnestic incapacitating effects.

Military

Iran's hybrid approach to warfare—using both conventional and unconventional capabilities—will pose a threat to U.S. interests in the region for the foreseeable future. Iran's unconventional warfare operations and network of militant partners and proxies enable Tehran to pursue its interests and maintain strategic depth with a modicum of deniability.

- Iran has started taking delivery of advanced trainer aircraft and probably will seek to acquire new conventional weapon systems, such as advanced fighter aircraft, helicopters, and main battle tanks. However, budgetary constraints will slow the pace and scale of acquisitions.

- Iran's missile, UAV, air defense, and naval capabilities will continue to threaten U.S. and partner commercial and military assets in the Middle East.

Iran's ballistic missile programs have the largest inventory in the region and Tehran is emphasizing improving the accuracy, lethality, and reliability of its missiles. Meanwhile, Iran's work on space launch vehicles (SLVs)—including its Simorgh—would shorten the timeline to produce an ICBM, if it decided to develop one, because the systems use similar technologies.

Cyber and Malign Influence Operations

Iran's growing expertise and willingness to conduct aggressive cyber operations make it a major threat to the security of U.S. and allied and partner networks and data. Tehran's opportunistic approach to cyber attacks puts U.S. infrastructure at risk for being targeted, particularly as its previous attacks against Israeli targets show that Iran is willing to target countries with stronger cyber capabilities than itself. Iran will continue to conduct malign influence operations in the Middle East and in other regions, including trying to undermine U.S. political processes and amplify discord.

Ahead of the U.S. election in 2024, Iran may attempt to conduct influence operations aimed at U.S. interests, including targeting U.S. elections, having demonstrated a willingness and capability to do so in the past.

- During the U.S. election cycle in 2020, Iranian cyber actors obtained or attempted to obtain U.S. voter information, sent threatening emails to voters, and disseminated disinformation about the election. The same Iranian actors have evolved their activities and developed a new set of techniques, combining cyber and influence capabilities, that Iran could deploy during the U.S. election cycle in 2024.

Challenges

Despite weathering protests in late 2022 and early 2023, Iran continues to face domestic challenges that constrain the regime's ability to achieve its goals. Mismanagement and international sanctions are brakes on the economy that limit the regime's ability to buy domestic support and legitimacy.

- Iran's economy continues to struggle amidst high inflation—likely to top 40 percent for 2023, sanctions pressure, and a depreciating currency. Most wages are unable to keep pace with the higher prices, leading to declines in households' spending power. During the coming years, Iran also will be increasingly challenged by climate change as water becomes scarcer.

- Iran's dependency on oil export revenues and slowing economic growth in China—Iran's largest buyer of oil—portend weaker revenues for Tehran and potentially higher budget deficits, probably forcing lower government spending on infrastructure, including for power and water.

- Iran's Supreme Leader, Ali Khamenei, has been serving in the position since 1989 and is in his mid-80s. His eventual passing could challenge a system characterized by elite factionalism that has only undergone a single supreme leader transition.

NORTH KOREA

Regional and Global Activities

North Korean leader Kim Jong Un will continue to pursue nuclear and conventional military capabilities that threaten the United States and its allies, which will enable periodic aggressive actions as he tries to reshape the regional security environment in his favor. North Korea has emerged from its deepest period of isolation driven by a combination of nearly two decades of severe UN sanctions and its self-imposed COVID-19 lockdown. Today, it is pursuing stronger ties with China and Russia with the goal of increasing financial gains, diplomatic support, and defense cooperation. Kim almost certainly has no intentions of negotiating away his nuclear program, which he perceives to be a guarantor of regime security and national pride. In addition, Kim probably hopes that he can use his bourgeoning defense ties with Russia to pursue his goal of achieving international acceptance as a nuclear power.

- In late 2023, Kim hosted high-level Chinese and Russian delegations in Pyongyang, and made his first trip overseas since the onset of the COVID-19 pandemic to meet with President Putin. Since this meeting, North Korea probably has begun shipping munitions to Russia in support of the conflict with Ukraine in exchange for diplomatic, economic, and military concessions.

- In response to strengthening trilateral cooperation between the United States, Japan, and South Korea, Pyongyang has sought to demonstrate the danger posed by its military through missile launches and rhetoric threatening nuclear retaliation. North Korea routinely times its missile launches and military demonstrations to counter U.S.–South Korea exercises in part to attempt to coerce both countries to change their behavior and counteract South Korean President Yoon Suk Yeol's hardline policies toward the North.

- North Korea increasingly will engage in illicit activities, including cyber theft labor deployments and the import and export of UN-proscribed commodities, to fund regime priorities such as the WMD program.

WMD

Kim remains strongly committed to expanding the country's nuclear weapons arsenal, which serves as the centerpiece of his national security structure.

- In March 2023, Kim ordered an increase in the nuclear weapons stockpile and the expansion of weapon-grade nuclear material production. North Korea also unveiled a purported tactical nuclear warhead and claimed it could be mounted on at least eight delivery systems, including an unmanned underwater vehicle and cruise missiles.

- North Korea has been prepared to resume nuclear tests at the Pungyye site since mid-2022.

North Korea maintains its CBW capabilities, and Pyongyang may use such weapons during a conflict or in an unconventional or clandestine attack.

Military

North Korea's military will pose a serious threat to the United States and its allies by its investment in niche capabilities designed to provide Kim with options to deter outside intervention, offset enduring deficiencies in the country's conventional forces, and advance his political objectives through coercion. Kim remains strongly committed to developing capabilities intended to challenge regional missile defense, diversify options to deliver nuclear warheads, and enhance second-strike capabilities.

- North Korea is working to develop its conventional capabilities, although testing and fielding occurs at a slower pace compared with developments in the missile force, given priority and systemic resource constraints. In 2023, North Korea showcased new UAV systems that appear similar to the U.S. MQ-9 Reaper and Global Hawk, though the technical capability probably is limited compared to the U.S. systems.

Kim will continue to prioritize efforts to build a more capable missile force—from cruise missiles through ICBMs, and hypersonic glide vehicles—designed to evade U.S. and regional missile defenses and imports a variety of dual-use goods in violation of UN sanctions, primarily from China and Russia.

- In 2023, North Korea launched its ballistic missile submarine following years of modifying an old Romeo-class submarine. Kim has stated his intention to convert more submarines for a similar mission.

- In January 2024, Pyongyang launched a new, solid-propellant missile that it claims is an intermediate-range ballistic missile equipped with a maneuverable, hypersonic reentry vehicle.

- In 2023, North Korea launched three SLVs, two failed and the third successfully placed a satellite in orbit.

- In 2023, North Korea conducted five flight tests of its ICBMs, including the Hwasong-15 and Hwasong-17 liquid-propellant ICBMs as well as its new solid-propellant ICBM, the Hwasong-18.

Cyber

North Korea's cyber program will pose a sophisticated and agile espionage, cybercrime, and attack threat. Pyongyang's cyber forces have matured and are fully capable of achieving a variety of strategic objectives against diverse targets, including a wider target set in the United States and South Korea.

North Korea will continue its ongoing cyber campaign, particularly cryptocurrency heists; seek a broad variety of approaches to launder and cash out stolen cryptocurrency; and maintain a program of IT workers serving abroad to earn additional funds.

Challenges

While North Korea has managed to weather the effects of the pandemic and its extreme self-imposed isolation; in the long term, Kim will have to balance his desire for absolute state control with the negative impact upon his country's economic well-being. The Kim regime has prioritized recentralizing authority above its population and its economy with brutal crackdowns and serious mismanagement of agriculture that probably are worsening living conditions. The North Korean regime has long feared losing control over its people and is trying to roll back the relatively modest levels of private economic activity that have arisen since the 1990s and to ensure state domination over everyday life.

- The regime's recentralization campaign is meant to ensure the long-term survival of Kim-family rule. Its intensity stems from the collapse of fellow communist dictatorships during the 1990s in which the gradual erosion of authority and infiltration of foreign ideas eventually undermined the state. The crackdown restricts livelihoods and promotes inefficient state controls, contributing to food shortages and some decline in civil order—particularly violent crime.

CONFLICTS AND FRAGILITY

Preface

The potential for interstate conflict and domestic turmoil in other countries around the world also continues to pose challenges for U.S. national security, both directly and as threats to our allies and partners. Rising tension and instability from these flashpoints can be exacerbated by the intensifying global power competition given the complex and interconnected security landscape. Conflicts, particularly those that disrupt global trade and investment flows, might lead to rising energy prices and increased economic fragility even in countries that are not directly involved or are far removed from the conflict. For example, tourism, which is a major foreign exchange earner for Egypt, Jordan, and Lebanon, has fallen sharply since the onset of the Gaza conflict and disruptions in Ukrainian food exports in 2022 helped to fuel rising global food prices. Regional and localized conflicts have far-reaching and sometimes cascading implications for not only neighboring countries, but also the world. In addition to being illustrative of this phenomenon, the ongoing conflict in Gaza also highlights the potential for spillover into larger and more dangerous conflict.

Gaza Conflict

The HAMAS attack against Israel in October 2023 and Israel's responding military campaign in Gaza has increased tensions throughout the region as Iranian proxies and partners conduct anti-U.S. and anti-Israel attacks, both in support of HAMAS and to pressure the United States. Media coverage of the destruction and loss of life are being amplified by active social media campaigns on all sides, roiling public reactions among neighboring countries and around the world. Israel will face mounting international pressure because of the dire humanitarian situation in the Gaza Strip, and Iranian-backed attacks will jeopardize stability in Lebanon, Iraq, the Gulf, and the Red Sea. The risk of escalation into direct interstate conflict, intended or otherwise, remains high.

- The Gaza conflict is posing a challenge to many key Arab partners, who face public sentiment against Israel and the United States for the death and destruction in Gaza, but also see the United States as the power broker best positioned to deter further aggression and end the conflict before it spreads deeper into the region.

Israel and Iran are trying to calibrate their actions against each other to avoid escalation into a direct full-scale conflict. We assess that Iranian leaders did not orchestrate nor had foreknowledge of the HAMAS attack against Israel.

Since October 2023, Iran has encouraged and enabled its various proxies and partners—including Hizballah, Iranian-backed groups in Iraq and Syria, and the Huthis in Yemen—to conduct strikes against Israeli or U.S. interests in the region.

- Hizballah is calibrating this pressure on Israel from the north while trying to avoid a broader war that would devastate Hizballah and Lebanon. Hizballah's leadership, though, probably will consider a range of retaliatory options depending on Israel's actions in Lebanon during the upcoming year.

- In Iraq, Iranian-aligned militias almost certainly will continue attacks against U.S. forces in Iraq and Syria.

- The Huthi's continued ballistic missile, cruise missile, and UAV attacks against merchant vessels transiting the Red Sea, which are disrupting international shipping, and on Israel create a real risk of broader escalation.

Both al-Qa'ida and ISIS, inspired by the HAMAS attack against Israel, have directed their supporters to conduct attacks against Israeli and U.S. interests. The HAMAS attack is encouraging individuals to conduct acts of antisemitic and Islamophobic terror worldwide and is galvanizing individuals to leverage the Palestinian plight for recruitment and inspiration to conduct attacks. The Nordic Resistance Movement—a transnational neo-Nazi organization—publicly praised the attack, illustrating the conflict's appeal to a range of threat actors.

In regard to Gaza, Jerusalem remains focused on destroying HAMAS, which its population broadly supports. Moreover, Israel probably will face lingering armed resistance from HAMAS for years to come, and the military will struggle to neutralize HAMAS's underground infrastructure, which allows insurgents to hide, regain strength, and surprise Israeli forces.

The governance and security structures in Gaza and the West Bank as well as the resolution of the humanitarian situation in Gaza and rebuilding will be key components of the long-term Israeli–Palestinian relationship.

- Israeli Prime Minister Binyamin Netanyahu has publicly stated his opposition to postwar diplomacy with the Palestinian Authority (PA) toward territorial compromise.

- Netanyahu's viability as leader as well as his governing coalition of far-right and ultraorthodox parties that pursued hardline policies on Palestinian and security issues may be in jeopardy. Distrust of Netanyahu's ability to rule has deepened and broadened across the public from its already high levels before the war, and we expect large protests demanding his resignation and new elections. A different, more moderate government is a possibility.

HAMAS's and the PA's continued animosity will be a factor in governance outcomes as will HAMAS's broad popular support. Much also will hinge on Israel's decisions regarding how to deal with Gaza in the aftermath of its campaign as well as scale and scope of its support for the PA.

Potential Interstate Conflict

Interstate conflict can have broader cascading security, economic, and humanitarian implications on a regional and even global scale. The following are a few of the potential conflicts between states that could spill over with repercussions that may require immediate U.S. attention.

China Maritime

Beijing's efforts to try to assert sovereignty claims over islands in the South and East China Seas will result in persistently high tension between the PRC and its neighboring competing claimants and increase opportunities for miscalculation, even though Beijing probably prefers to avoid direct conflict. Beijing maintains a maritime presence near contested areas, and its military bases in the Spratly Islands allow for a sustained presence in disputed areas and provide the capability to rapidly react to crises in the South China Sea.

- In 2023, the PRC Coast Guard used water cannons and floating barriers to block Filipino access to disputed areas in the South China Sea. The PRC's collisions with Filipino supply ships generated media attention that highlighted China's aggressive behaviors. Manila is unlikely to relinquish its outpost at Second Thomas Shoal presenting more opportunities for inadvertent escalation by either side.

- Tension between China and Japan over the Senkaku Islands last flared up a decade ago. Since then, Chinese ships have constantly remained in the proximity of the disputed islands, occasionally entering the territorial zone, and driving responses from Japan's Self-Defense Force to monitor the activity.

India–China

The shared disputed border between India and China will remain a strain on their bilateral relationship. While the two sides have not engaged in significant cross-border clashes since 2020, they are maintaining large troop deployments, and sporadic encounters between opposing forces risk miscalculation and escalation into armed conflict.

India–Pakistan

New Delhi and Islamabad are inclined to sustain the current fragile calm in their relationship following their renewal of a cease-fire along the Line of Control in early 2021. However, neither side has used this period of calm to rebuild their bilateral ties as each government has focused on more pressing domestic priorities including election perpetrations and campaigning and for Pakistan, concerns over rising militant attacks in its west. Pakistan's long history of supporting anti-India militant groups and India's increased willingness, under the leadership of Prime Minister Narendra Modi, to respond with military force to perceived or real Pakistani provocations raise the risk of escalation during a crisis. There remains the potential for an event to trigger a rapid escalation.

Azerbaijan–Armenia

Relations between Armenia and Azerbaijan are likely to remain tense, but Azerbaijan's retaking of Nagorno-Karabakh (N-K) has reduced volatility, and a military confrontation probably would be limited in duration and intensity. Nevertheless, the lack of a bilateral peace treaty, the proximity of their military forces, the lack of a cease-fire enforcement mechanism, and Azerbaijan's readiness to use calibrated military pressure to advance its goals in talks with Armenia will remain. Moreover, the transition of N-K governance from ethnic Armenians to Azerbaijanis and Azerbaijan's demand for access to a land corridor linking Azerbaijan to its exclave will elevate the risk of armed confrontation.

- In September 2023, Azerbaijan initiated a military operation that led to the defeat of the N-K Self Defense Force and the surrender of the de facto N-K authorities. The rapid exodus of most of the region's ethnic Armenian population and the planned self-dissolution of the government allowed Baku to advance plans to integrate the region with Azerbaijan, effectively removing this longstanding issue from the bilateral peace agenda.

Potential Intrastate Turmoil

Intrastate turmoil—whether grounded in domestic unrest, economic discontent, or governance challenges—can fuel cycles of violence, insurgencies, and internal conflict. The challenges often are intertwined with diminished socioeconomic performance, endemic corruption, population dislocations, pressures from climate change, and the spread of extremists' ideologies from terrorist and insurgent groups. During the past decade, an erosion of democracy around the world, strains in U.S. alliances, and challenges to international norms have made it more difficult for the United States and its allies to tackle global issues while creating greater opportunities for rogue governments and groups to operate with impunity. Below we highlight a few instances that will have the potential for greater impact on global security and the potential for action from the United States, its allies, and partners.

The Balkans

The Western Balkans probably will face an increased risk of localized interethnic violence during 2024. Nationalist leaders are likely to exacerbate tension for their political advantage and outside actors will reinforce and exploit ethnic differences to increase or protect their regional influence or thwart greater Balkan integration into the EU or Euro–Atlantic institutions.

- Clashes between Serb nationalists and Kosovar authorities have led to deaths and injuries, including injuries to NATO peacekeepers, in 2023.

- Bosnian Serb leader Milorad Dodik is taking provocative steps to neutralize international oversight in Bosnia and secure de facto secession for his Republika Srpska. His action could prompt leaders of the Bosniak (Bosnian Muslim) population to bolster their own capacity to protect their interests and possibly lead to violent conflicts that could overwhelm peacekeeping forces.

Afghanistan

The Taliban regime has strengthened its power in Afghanistan, suppressed anti-Taliban groups, bolstered international engagement, and will continue to prioritize enforcement of theocratic rule. However, the Taliban will not adequately address Afghanistan's persistent humanitarian crisis or structural economic weaknesses.

- The Taliban will continue to implement restrictive measures, carry out public punishments, crack down on protests, and prevent most women and girls from attending secondary school and university. However, near-term prospects for regime-threatening resistance remain low because large swathes of the Afghan public are weary of war and fearful of Taliban reprisals, and armed remnants lack strong leadership and external support.

- Regional powers will continue to focus largely on keeping problems contained in Afghanistan and seek to develop transactional arrangements with the Taliban while proceeding cautiously with Taliban requests for formal recognition.

Sudan

Prolonged conflict heightens the risks of conflict spreading beyond Sudan's borders, external actors joining the fray, and civilians facing death and displacement. The Sudanese Armed Forces and Rapid Support Forces are still fighting because their leaders calculate that they can achieve their goals absent a negotiated cessation of hostilities. With Sudan at the crossroads of the Horn of Africa, the Sahel, and North Africa, it could once again become an ideal environment for terrorist and criminal networks.

- Sudan's warring security forces may be receiving more foreign military support, which is likely to hamper progress on any future peace talks. Any increased involvement by one external actor could prompt others to quickly follow suit.

Ethiopia

Ethiopia is undergoing multiple, simultaneous internal conflicts, heightening interethnic tension and the risk of atrocities against civilians. A new conflict emerged in the Amhara Regional State in April 2023, when the Ethiopian Government clashed with Amhara militia and fighting persisted throughout the year. While the Cessation of Hostilities Agreement in November 2022 between the Ethiopian Government and the Tigrayans ended a two-year war, unresolved territorial issues could lead to a resumption of conflict.

The Sahel

Since 2020, the Sahel has experienced seven irregular transfers of power because leaders have failed to address poor governance and public grievances or adequately resourced their militaries to achieve their missions. This turmoil raises the likelihood that these crises will metastasize and spillover to neighboring countries in Coastal West Africa in 2024. Many Coastal West African governments are facing potential coups because of lingering civil-military strains, growing public dissatisfaction with their failure to deliver improved governance and living standards, and an increase in foreign partners willing to condone military rule to focus on narrow security interests. Future coup leaders most likely will calculate that competition among major powers will create the space to weather any international fallout.

- Russia has opportunistically capitalized on domestic turmoil, offering rhetorical and, in some instances, substantive support to those seeking to oust regimes.

- Mounting crises are beginning to fray regional institutions, further hampering their ability to develop effective regional security responses. In 2023, juntas in Burkina Faso, Mali, and Niger formed a separate alliance to buck pressure from the Economic Community of West African

States (ECOWAS), historically one of the most consistent bodies in trying to uphold anti-coup norms in the region.

- Several Western partners are focusing on core security interests in the region—such as stemming migrant flows, containing geopolitical rivals, and CT gains—at the expense of longer-term support to democracy and governance.

Haiti

Conditions will remain unpredictable as weak government institutions lose their grip on power to gang territorial control, particularly in the capital Port-au-Prince. This will be coupled with an eroding economy, infrastructure, and an increasingly dire humanitarian situation. Gangs will be more likely to violently resist a foreign national force deployment to Haiti because they perceive it to be a shared threat to their control and operations.

- Top Haitian gang leaders such as G-9 leader Jimmy "Barbeque" Cherizier and Kraze Barye leader Vitelhomme Innocent have called for the overthrow of Prime Minister Ariel Henry's government.

- The Haitian National Police has been unable to counter gang violence and has been plagued by resource issues, corruption challenges, and limited training.

Venezuela

Disputed Venezuelan President Nicolas Maduro will retain a solid hold on power and is unlikely to lose the 2024 presidential election because of his control of state institutions that influence the electoral process and his willingness to exercise his power. The opposition, which has often been divided, holds few public positions of influence.

- Support from China, Iran, and Russia help the Maduro regime evade sanctions.

- So far, the regime has banned top opposition candidates from holding public office, restricted media coverage of opposition politicians, and placed close allies in the National Electoral Council to ensure Maduro's victory while also trying to avoid blatant voting fraud.

More than 7.7 million Venezuelans have left the country since 2017, 6.5 million of whom are living in Latin America and the Caribbean. Venezuelan emigration to the region and the United States is likely to remain elevated through next year as the lack of economic opportunities are likely to persist.

- More than 80 percent of Venezuelans have incomes below the poverty line and low-levels of economic growth would be insufficient to lift most out of poverty or mitigate drivers of migration.

TRANSNATIONAL ISSUES

PREFACE

Transnational threats interact in a complex system along with threats from state-actors, often reinforcing each other and creating compounding and cascading risks to U.S. national security. Increasing interconnections among countries also have created new opportunities for transnational interference and conflict. Several clear and direct challenges are the rapid development of technologies, the spread of repression beyond physical borders, the threats posed by transnational organized crime and terrorism, and the societal effects of international migration.

CONTESTED SPACES

Disruptive Technology

New technologies—particularly in the fields of AI and biotechnology—are being developed and are proliferating at a rate that makes it challenging for companies and governments to shape norms regarding civil liberties, privacy, and ethics. The convergence of these emerging technologies is likely to create breakthroughs, which could lead to the rapid development of asymmetric threats—such as advanced UAVs—to U.S. interests and probably will help shape U.S. economic prosperity.

- For example, stealth technology has significantly impacted conventional defense systems and has driven the efforts of varying countries to start a new round of research on detection systems and guided weapons. A key trend is the development of advanced materials with enhanced stealth properties with reduced reflection and absorption properties.

Advances in AI and new machine learning models are moving AI into its industrial age, with potentially huge economic impacts for both winners and followers and unintended consequences—from rampant deepfakes and misinformation to the development of AI-generated computer viruses or new chemical weapons. Generative AI is a means for discovering and designing novel technologies and advanced system-level processes that could strengthen a country's technological, economic, and broader strategic competitiveness.

- China is pursuing AI for smart cities, mass surveillance, healthcare, drug discovery, and intelligent weapons platforms. Chinese AI firms are already world leaders in voice and image recognition, video analytics, and mass surveillance technologies.

- PRC researchers have described the application of generative AI to drug discovery as "revolutionary." On average, it takes more than 10 years and billions of dollars to develop a new drug. AI can make drug discovery faster and cheaper by using machine-learning models to predict how potential drugs might behave in the body and cut down on the need for painstaking lab work on dead-end compounds.

- Russia is using AI to create deepfakes and is developing the capability to fool experts. Individuals in warzones and unstable political environments may serve as some of the highest-value targets for such deepfake malign influence.

Innovators in synthetic biology probably will control new military and commercial applications and hold trillions of dollars in production capacity, including supply chains for products that vary from disease-resistant crop seeds to metals to pharmaceuticals.

- Countries, such as China and the United States, that lead biotechnological breakthroughs in fields such as precision medicine, synthetic biology, big data, and biomimetic materials, will not only drive industry growth, but also international competition and will exert substantial influence over the global economy for generations.

Digital Authoritarianism and Transnational Repression

Foreign states are advancing digital and physical means to repress individual critics and diaspora communities abroad, including in the United States, to limit their influence over domestic publics. States are also growing more sophisticated in digital influence operations that try to affect foreign publics' views, sway voters' perspectives, shift policies, and create social and political upheaval. Digital technologies have become a core component of many governments' repressive toolkits even as they continue to engage in physical acts of transnational repression, including assassinations, abductions, abuse of arrest warrants and familial intimidation. The PRC probably is the top perpetrator of physical transnational repression.

- During the next several years, governments are likely to exploit new and more intrusive technologies—including generative AI—for transnational repression. From 2011 to 2023, at least 74 countries contracted with private companies to obtain commercial spyware, which governments are increasingly using to target dissidents and journalists.

- PRC expatriates have faced accusations of false bomb threats in countries around the world, resulting in local police investigations, revoked visas, placement on travel blacklists, and sometimes detention, as means to harass dissidents overseas. The PRC also probably will seek to maintain its public security bureaus also known as "overseas police stations" to monitor and repress the Chinese diaspora.

WMD

Nuclear Weapons

The expansion of nuclear weapons stockpiles and their delivery systems, coupled with increasing regional conflicts involving nuclear weapons states, pose a significant challenge to global efforts to prevent the spread and use of nuclear weapons. Arms control efforts through 2035 will change in scope and complexity as the number of strategic technologies and the countries that have them grow.

- China and Russia are seeking to ensure strategic stability with the United States through the growth and development of a range of weapons capabilities, including nontraditional weapons intended to defeat or evade U.S. missile defenses.

- North Korea continues to threaten to conduct a seventh nuclear test and the potential for heightened tension between Pakistan and India could increase the risk of nuclear escalation.

Chemical Weapons

The use of chemical weapons, particularly in situations other than state-on-state military operations, could increase in the near future. During the past decade, state and non-state actors have used chemical warfare agents in a range of scenarios, including the Syrian military's use of chlorine and sarin against opposition groups and civilians, and North Korea's and Russia's use of chemical agents in targeted killings. More state actors could use chemicals in operations against dissidents, defectors, and other perceived enemies of the state; protestors under the guise of quelling domestic unrest; or against their own civilian or refugee populations.

Biological Weapons

Current biological agents and rapidly advancing biotechnology underscore the diverse and dynamic nature of deliberate biological threats. Rapid advances in dual-use technology, including bioinformatics, synthetic biology, nanotechnology, and genomic editing, could enable development of novel biological threats.

- Russia, China, Iran, and North Korea probably maintain the capability to produce and use pathogens and toxins, and China and Russia have proven adept at manipulating the information space to reduce trust and confidence in countermeasures and U.S. biotechnology and research.

SHARED DOMAINS

Environmental Change and Extreme Weather

The risks to U.S. national security interests are increasing as the physical effects of climate and environmental change intersect with geopolitical tension and vulnerabilities of some global systems. Climate-related disasters in low-income countries will deepen economic challenges, raise the risk of inter-communal conflict over scarce resources, and increase the need for humanitarian and financial assistance.

- Climate-related disasters and economic losses in low-income countries are poised to continue contributing to cross-border migration.

- Competition over access and economic resources in the Arctic, as sea ice recedes, increases the risk of miscalculation, particularly while there is military tension between Russia and the other seven countries with Arctic territory.

- El Nino weather patterns are combining with the effects of climate change and pre-existing vulnerabilities in critical infrastructure to worsen populations' exposure to flooding, drought, heatwaves, and intense storms. El Nino-related events are projected to reduce global economic growth, resulting in more than $3 trillion in lost GDP during the rest of the decade.

- Droughts are decreasing shipping capacity and energy generation in Central America, China, Europe, and the United States, and insurance losses from catastrophes have increased 250 percent during the past 30 years.

- Changing weather patterns' effects on major agricultural exporters and important local agricultural areas may put more stress on food systems in vulnerable areas of Africa, Latin America, and South Asia. The sustainable fish stocks on which some coastal populations depend are declining because of rising ocean temperatures and overfishing, particularly by illegal, unreported, and unregulated (IUU) fishing.

Intensifying effects of climate change—combined with El Nino weather patterns—are likely to exacerbate risks to human health, primarily but not exclusively, in low- and middle-income countries. Rising land and ocean temperatures, changing precipitation patterns, and increased frequency of severe weather events are likely to intersect with environmental degradation, pollution, and poor resource management to exacerbate food and water insecurity, malnutrition, and disease outbreaks.

Health Security

National health system shortfalls, public mistrust and medical misinformation, and eroding global health governance will impede the capacity of countries to respond to health threats. Countries remain vulnerable to the introduction of a new or reemerging pathogen that could cause another devastating pandemic.

- The predicted shortage of at least 10 million healthcare workers by 2030 will occur primarily in low- and middle-income countries.

- Global health governance and adherence to UN health protocols may be eroded during the coming year by continued disregard by governments of international health institutions and norms and adversary interference in global health initiatives.

- Drivers for infectious disease emergence are on the rise, including deforestation, wildlife harvesting and trade, mass food production, and lack of international consensus on biosafety norms. These drivers are compounded by factors that facilitate global spread, such as international travel and trade, inadequate global disease surveillance and control, weakened health systems, public distrust, and medical misinformation.

- Significant outbreaks of highly pathogenic avian influenza, cholera, dengue, Ebola, monkeypox, and polio have stretched global and national disease detection and response systems further straining the international community's ability to address health emergencies.

Our Assessment of the Origins of COVID-19

The IC continues to investigate how SARS-CoV-2, the virus that causes COVID-19, first infected humans. All agencies assess two hypotheses are plausible: natural exposure to an infected animal and a laboratory-associated incident.

- The National Intelligence Council and four other IC agencies assess that the initial human infection with SARS-CoV-2 most likely was caused by natural exposure to an infected animal that carried SARS-CoV-2 or a close progenitor, a virus that probably would be more than 99 percent similar to SARSCoV-2. The Department of Energy and the FBI assess that a laboratory-associated incident was the most likely cause of the first human infection with SARS-CoV-2, although for different reasons. The CIA and another agency remain unable to determine the precise origin of the COVID-19 pandemic, as both hypotheses rely on significant assumptions or face challenges with conflicting reporting.

- Beijing continues to resist sharing critical and technical information about coronaviruses and to blame other countries, including the United States, for the pandemic.

Anomalous Health Incidents

We continue to closely examine anomalous health incidents (AHIs), particularly in areas we have identified as requiring additional research and analysis. Most IC agencies have concluded that it is very unlikely a foreign adversary is responsible for the reported AHIs. IC agencies have varying confidence levels because we still have gaps given the challenges collecting on foreign adversaries—as we do on many issues involving them. As part of its review, the IC identified critical assumptions surrounding the initial AHIs reported in Cuba from 2016 to 2018, which framed the IC's understanding of this phenomenon, but were not borne out by subsequent medical and technical analysis. In light of this and the evidence that points away from a foreign adversary, causal mechanism, or unique syndromes linked to AHIs, IC agencies assess those symptoms reported by U.S. personnel probably were the result of factors that did not involve a foreign adversary.

- These findings do not call into question the very real experiences and symptoms that our colleagues and their family members have reported. We continue to prioritize our work on such incidents, allocating resources and expertise across the government, pursuing multiple lines of inquiry and seeking information to fill the gaps we have identified.

Migration

Conflict, violence, political instability, poor economic conditions, and natural disasters will continue to displace growing numbers of people within their own national borders and internationally—straining countries' capacity to absorb new arrivals and governments' abilities to provide services and manage domestic public discontent. The Western Hemisphere most likely will continue to sustain high levels of intra-regional migrant flows driven by poor socioeconomic conditions and insecurity as well as pull factors that include economic opportunity, family reunification, and perceptions of immigration policies in recipient or transit countries.

- The number of individuals internally displaced from their homes in 2022 was more than three times higher than the average of the previous 10 years. Irregular migration to high-income countries is increasing as several countries in Africa, Latin America, and the Caribbean experience political turmoil and poor economic performance.

- Political repression and lack of economic opportunities will continue to drive Cuban, Nicaraguan, and Venezuelan emigration; however, those regimes will continue to blame U.S. sanctions and policies for irregular emigration from their countries.

- Changes to Western Hemisphere countries' visa requirements—such as Nicaragua's relaxation of requirements for nationals from Haiti—could trigger new surges in U.S.-bound irregular migration.

NON-STATE ACTOR ISSUES

Transnational Organized Crime

Transnational criminal organizations (TCOs) threaten U.S. and allied public health systems, exploit the international financial system, and degrade the safety and security of the United States and partner nations. TCOs incite instability and violence, drive migration, and provide some U.S. adversaries with additional avenues to advance their geopolitical interests.

Foreign Illicit Drugs

Western Hemisphere-based TCOs involved in illicit drug production and trafficking bound for the United States and partner nations, endanger the health and safety of millions of individuals and contribute to a global health crisis. Illicit drugs including fentanyl, heroin, methamphetamine, and South American-sourced cocaine all contribute to global demand for drugs.

- Mexico-based TCOs are the dominant producers and suppliers of illicit drugs to the U.S. market, including fentanyl, heroin, methamphetamine, and South American-sourced cocaine.

- Both Colombia and Ecuador are impacted by record levels of cocaine being produced and trafficked to international markets contributing to a global drug demand, while fueling drug related violence within their borders.

Fentanyl

Illicit fentanyl will continue to pose a major threat to the health of Americans. In 2023, a majority of the more than 100,000 annual drug overdose deaths in the United States are attributed to illicit fentanyl mostly supplied by Mexican-based TCOs, even as U.S. law enforcement seized record amounts of illicit fentanyl, precursor chemicals, and pill pressing equipment.

- Mexico-based TCOs are the dominant producers of illicit fentanyl for the U.S. market, although there also are independent illicit fentanyl producers, and the fragmentation of fentanyl operations has made disruption efforts challenging. Some aspects of fentanyl production are spilling over into the United States with drug traffickers conducting the finishing stages of fentanyl pill packing or pressing in the United States.

- China remains the primary source for illicit fentanyl precursor chemicals and pill pressing equipment. Brokers circumvent international controls through mislabeled shipments and the purchase of unregulated dual-use chemicals. However, Mexico-based TCOs also are sourcing precursor chemicals to a lesser extent from other nations such as India.

Money Laundering and Financial Crimes

TCOs are defrauding individuals, businesses, and government programs, while laundering billions of dollars of illicit proceeds through U.S. financial institutions. Their fraud schemes and tactics vary widely. Some use shell and front companies to obfuscate their illicit activities and some TCOs rely on professional money launderers or financial experts and other tactics to launder illicit proceeds.

- TCOs still rely on traditional money laundering methods and bulk cash smuggling operations to repatriate drug proceeds from the United States, while some money launderers are using cryptocurrency transactions.

Cyber Crime

Transnational organized criminals involved in ransomware operations are improving their attacks, extorting funds, disrupting critical services, and exposing sensitive data. Important U.S. services and critical infrastructure such as health care, schools, and manufacturing continue to experience ransomware attacks; however, weak cyber defenses, coupled with efforts to digitize economies, have made low-income countries' networks also attractive targets.

- The emergence of inexpensive and anonymizing online infrastructure combined with the growing profitability of ransomware has led to the proliferation, decentralization, and specialization of cyber criminal activity. This interconnected system has improved the efficiency and sophistication of ransomware attacks while also lowering the technical bar for entry for new actors.

- Transnational organized criminals sometimes cease operations temporarily in response to high-profile attention, law enforcement action, or disruption of infrastructure, although group members also find ways to rebrand, reconstitute, or renew their activities.

- Absent cooperative law enforcement from Russia or other countries that provide cyber criminals a safe haven or permissive environment, mitigation efforts will remain limited.

Undermining Rule of Law

TCOs and criminal gangs undermine the rule of law through exploiting corruption networks, committing acts of violence, and overpowering regional security forces. TCOs regularly co-opt foreign government officials through bribes or threats to create a permissive operating environment and target officials who support stronger counter-drug efforts.

- TCOs bribe foreign political candidates and security officials in an effort to limit enforcement actions and to protect illicit operations, such as illicit drug production or cross-border smuggling operations.

- Drug-related gang violence in Ecuador has led to surging homicide rates and the assassination of a presidential candidate. The nation has declared multiple states of emergency, suspending essential public services—including public transportation—and closing schools and businesses.

Human Trafficking

TCOs and criminal actors view human trafficking, including sex trafficking and forced labor, as low risk crimes of opportunity. Multiple criminal actors engage in operations that seek to exploit vulnerable individuals and groups to bolster illicit revenue streams. TCOs that engage in human trafficking may also engage in drug trafficking, weapons smuggling, human smuggling, and money laundering.

- Human traffickers typically coerce or defraud their victims into sex trafficking or forced labor, confiscating identification documents and requiring the payment of debts. In 2023, U.S. law enforcement officials noted multiple incidents where unaccompanied minors were exploited in forced labor operations in U.S. food processing plants to pay off debts.

- TCOs based in the Western Hemisphere and Asia are most likely to engage in human trafficking activity with ties to the United States.

Migrants transiting the Western Hemisphere to the United States are exploited by criminal actors through kidnapping for ransom, targets of forced labor, or victims of sex trafficking operations. TCOs, human smugglers, gangs, and lone criminal actors are all taking advantage of elevated levels of U.S.-bound migration, and vulnerable migrants are at risk of being trafficked.

- Some migrants, who voluntarily use human smuggling networks to facilitate their travel to the United States, are trafficked during their journey.

Global Terrorism

U.S. persons and interests at home and abroad will face an ideologically diverse threat from terrorism. This threat is mostly likely to manifest in small cells or individuals inspired by foreign terrorist organizations and violent extremist ideologies to conduct attacks. While al-Qa'ida has reached an operational nadir in Afghanistan and Pakistan and ISIS has suffered cascading leadership losses in Iraq and Syria, regional affiliates will continue to expand. These gains symbolize the shift of the center of gravity in the Sunni global jihad to Africa.

- Terrorists will maintain an interest in conducting attacks using chemical, biological and radioactive materials against U.S. persons, allies, and interests worldwide. Terrorists from diverse ideological backgrounds continue to circulate instructions of varied credibility for the procurement or production of toxic or radioactive weapons using widely available materials in social media and online fora.

ISIS

ISIS will remain a centralized global organization even as it has been forced to rely on regional branches in response to successive leadership losses during the past few years. External capabilities vary across ISIS's global branches, but the group will remain focused on attempting to conduct and inspire global attacks against the West and Western interests.

- ISIS–Greater Sahara and ISIS–West Africa contribute to and capitalize on government instability, communal conflict, and anti-government grievances to make gains in Nigeria and the Sahel.

- ISIS-Khorasan is trying to conduct attacks that undermine the legitimacy of the Taliban regime by expanding attacks against foreign interests in Afghanistan.

Al-Qaʻida

Al-Qaʻida's regional affiliates on the African continent and Yemen will sustain the global network as the group maintains its strategic intent to target the United States and U.S. citizens. Al-Qaʻida senior leadership has not yet announced the replacement for the former emir, Ayman al-Zawahiri, reflecting the regionally focused and decentralized nature of the organization.

- Al-Shabaab continues to advance its attack capabilities by acquiring weapons systems while countering a multinational CT campaign, presenting a risk to U.S. personnel. In 2023, al-Shabaab also expanded its operations in Northeast Kenya.

Hizballah

Lebanese Hizballah will continue to develop its global terrorist capabilities as a complement to the group's growing conventional military capabilities in the region. Since October 2023, Hizballah has conducted attacks along Israel's northern border to tie down Israeli forces as they seek to eliminate HAMAS in Gaza. Hizballah probably will continue to conduct provocative actions such as rocket launches against Israel throughout the conflict.

- Hizballah seeks to limit U.S. influence in Lebanon and the broader Middle East, and maintains the capability to target U.S. persons and interests in the region, worldwide, and, to a lesser extent, in the United States.

Transnational Racially or Ethnically Motivated Violent Extremists

The transnational racially or ethnically motivated violent extremists (RMVE) movement, in particular motivated by white supremacy, will continue to foment violence across Europe, South America, Australia, Canada, and New Zealand inspiring the lone actor or small-cell attacks that pose a significant threat to U.S. persons. The loose structure of transnational RMVE organizations and networks, which encourage or inspire but do not typically direct attacks, will challenge local security services and creates resilience against disruptions.

- Lone actors are difficult to detect and disrupt because of their lack of affiliation. While these violent extremists tend to leverage simple attack methods, they can have devastating, outsized consequences.

- RMVE publications and manifestoes from previous attackers feed the RMVE movement with violent propaganda, targets, and tactics. The Terrorgram Collective, a loosely connected network of online channels and chatrooms, has a global reach and with its sophisticated online publications seek to inspire violence.

- Since early 2022, we have identified five RMVE attacks and five suspected RMVE attacks, killing a total of 27 people, by apparent lone actors in the United States and abroad. During the same period, there have been disrupted RMVE plots, arrests, and threats reported in several European countries.

Private Military and Security Companies

PMSCs are a growing presence in the international environment, and a handful of these firms associated with U.S. rivals, such as Russia, threaten global security in many countries and regions through their ability to potentially foment violence and escalate instability in already fragile regions

- PMSCs have become an essential component of modern military operations and the demand for their services is likely to grow. The largest part of the industry are corporations who provide for-hire security services for commercial interests or states. However, China, Russia, Turkey, and the UAE see PMSCs as a valuable tool in their arsenal for either advancing or protecting their interests abroad.

- Many governments will look to PMSCs to play an important role as a force multiplier for their conventional militaries—filling highly technical or manpower-intensive tasks such as maintenance, logistics, or fixed site security—or in some cases providing highly specialized, turn-key direct-action capabilities absent in their forces.

- Only a small number of PMSC contracts involve direct intervention, which are high-risk activities that may require the application of deadly force.

- No other PMSC has the funding sources, training, and size to operate on Vagner's scale as a proxy force, although a state actor could similarly scale a smaller PMSC's activities within one to two years.

www.ingramcontent.com/pod-product-compliance
Lightning Source LLC
Chambersburg PA
CBHW081926170426
43200CB00014B/2844